# HOW TO SAW WOOD
# WITH AN ANGEL

# HOW TO SAW WOOD WITH AN ANGEL

Gertrude Story

Thistledown Press Ltd.

© Gertrude Story, 1992
Large Print Edition, 1994
All Rights Reserved

Story, Gertrude, 1929-
How to saw wood with an angel
ISBN 1-895449-31-6

I. Large type books.   I. Title.

PS8587.T677H68  1994   C813'.54   C94-920074-3
PR9199.3.S767H68  1994

Book design by A.M. Forrie
Cover art by K. Gwen Frank
Typeset in 16 pt. Century Old Style by Thistledown Press Ltd.

Printed and bound in Canada by
Webcom Printing
Scarborough, Ontario

Thistledown Press Ltd.
633 Main Street
Saskatoon, Saskatchewan   S7H 0J8

Acknowledgements

The John Masefield quotation is from *Shakespeare and the Spiritual Life* (Clarendon Press, Oxford, 1924).
The quotation from Jalal-ad-Din ar-Rumi is from the *Mathnawi,* a Sufi text.
Also mentioned are the *Canadian Encyclopedia* (Hurtig Publishers Ltd., Edmonton, 1985) and the *Funk & Wagnalls Dictionary,* Canadian Edition (Fitzhenry and Whiteside, Toronto, 1974).

This book has been published with the assistance of The Canada Council, the Saskatchewan Arts Board and a grant from the National Library of Canada.

*For anyone who has ever said,
"I wish somebody would dedicate
a book to me, sometime!"*

*and for
(chronologically speaking)
Brian Hugh, Ellen Louise, Joseph James, Anna
Maureen, Maureen Elizabeth, and Daniel Joseph:
my reasons for being.*

# CONTENTS

How to Saw Wood with an Angel   11

Falling into Winter   29

Moose Jaw, and Jitneys, and the *Saturday Evening Post*   38

Northward, Ho!   45

Protesting the Protestant Work Ethic   60

The Sounds of Silence   71

Doing Co-operation   77

The Way Spring Springs to Mind   81

The Trouble with Angels Is   90

Free-Traded Thanksgiving   100

End of Steel   108

Wow, Saskatoons!   111

Country Road, Take Me Home, or Else!   122

Talkin' Prairie   136

Pigweed, Pigs, and Other Pretty Surprises   161

The Power of Deer   173

Following the Bliss of Weirdos   188

# How to Saw Wood with an Angel

I've always kind of wanted to write a How To book. Well, if I had to write a book at all. I never really "burned" in that appropriate literary Hemingway-and-the-road-to-the-faggot-pile way to spill out the truths of human heart and mind as learned in a two-bodies' sleeping bag on the top of a stark mountain somewhere, though the Other One who lives inside my head seems to have danced to that tune a time or two. As far as I'm concerned the writing of books is the seminal incompatability between mind and spirit, between "that other one" and me as I know me. Books, for one thing, rarely make the writer a bagful of money.

But once I found out that How To books, including How To Cook books, gave you a better base from which to buy your SaskPower and your groceries, it sort of piqued my curiosity — in an experimental way, that is. Except for having to support my few but unfortunate bad habits, I'm not all that interested in writing *any* kind of book, including this one.

And so, when I wanted to know if I'd be able to buy some SaskPower power this coming winter to help the big old wood stove keep this little old house passably warm, I put the question directly into the hands of Holy Spirit. I did so upon direct instructions from the Inner Plane (I hope I'm sounding Shirley MacLaine-ish enough to grab you here) and in my particular case that means from an entire gaggle of not-afraid-to-speak-up Teachers-of-Mind.

When I had put the question of SaskPower, the household budget, and prospective winter goose bumps raised over the entire surface of a more-than-sixty-year-old body into the hands of Holy Spirit, Holy Spirit spoke up on the Inner Plane and said, "How the hell should *I* know?"

So much for the still, small voice so much touted in the annals of the universal Esoteric!

All the same, I have not survived on this peculiar little planet for sixty years and-then-some without learning a thing or two. So I sat down one day and I wrote to the publisher of *The Last House on Main Street,* which is the seventh book to have helped me buy a winter's worth of SaskPower, and I asked the publisher's collective mind if it might be interested in a kind of sequel to that book.

That seemed to make a very short letter. And short letters do not "set," aesthetically, on the computer page format I am currently stuck with, largely because I do not know enough about the computer that has bull-dozed its way into my life. Eventually, I trust, I shall be able to inveigle my one and only son-in-law, a certified C.C.F. (Committed Computer Freak), into coming up to my place to rearrange the bits and bytes in a way that won't bite my head or letterhead off. In the meantime, I am stuck with it.

To fill up the page of this too-short letter to the publisher it suddenly seemed a pretty good notion to give some idea about the stories that would be included in such a book. The number of stories written and ready for the undertaking were, well ... zero. So there were no samples to send along. But hey, what about titles? Titles are always good. Titles are often the last thing a writer comes up with, so if the titles are there, she must have the stories, right?

Well, as it happens, I live with a Writer Inside. I don't mean by that that I myself am generally to be found doing chores and things *outside* the house while, at the same time, there is someone else *inside* the house busily writing and, perhaps, occasionally making a little potato-onion soup for when I'm done with the outside chores and the writer is done with the inside work.

What I mean by this Writer Inside is the someone who seems to live somewhere on the Inner Planes. (*Forget* Shirley MacLaine now, OK? Shirley MacLaine does not know everything there is to know about this kind of stuff, and the way I'm telling it to you is the way it really is, at least with me!) This Writer Inside lives maybe within that creative Right-Hand Mind so many people are talking about, and writing books about, and holding seminars about — or, more correctly, holding seminars out of. Anyway, somewhere there abides The Writer Inside who presents the words for stories — stories told as well as stories written, for The Writer Inside is not at all fussy to know what you are going to do with them, It only wants to know: All right now, are you going to be a good girl today for once and *listen* to the words that *I* have to tell you?

And The Writer Inside me (let us call It *She*) happens to consider She is really hot on titles. I myself am lousy in that department.... So as soon as I mentioned titles for non-existent stories in a non-existent book, bingo! there they were, a whole raft of them.

The first one was the one at the beginning of this story.

I expect The Writer Inside was pretty sure the publisher would say *Heck, no* to the book and so She would never have to come up with the stories, only this gaggle of titles, see? I'm not even going to tell you the names of the rest of them, in case this smart alec Writer Inside cannot deliver them as the project progresses. All I'll say is there will be the very devil to pay if she presents the one with the devil in it.

So.

Well, we got a letter back from the publisher. Or I should say a note; publishers are more into notes than letters of late, I have noticed. Unless maybe for form letters. They are rather fond, really, of form letters — who can blame them? Especially of the ones that say, very nicely, No thank you! Anyway, we got this: "Yes, hey, we can hardly wait to read the one about the purple-shoed devil" and so The Writer Inside got stuck with the whole mess. Serves Her right; there's a penalty to be paid, always, for being too creative.

Well, it's no skin off my nose, to put it not-too-delicately. It will be interesting to see what She comes up with, this Writer Inside, for this *How to Saw Wood with an Angel.*

*Wait, wait, wait, now! Once you have issued the challenge to The Writer Inside and, therefore, to The System of All Things, you must sit quietly within your own sweet doubting self, and listen! And, once the words start coming, you must do your part by getting them down. Getting them down before they disappear, hey, that's the* real *trick!*

Aha!

*Matthew, Mark, Luke and John*
*Guard the bed I lie upon;*
*Guard the foot and guard the head:*
*Guardian angels for my bed.*

That, as nearly as I can remember it, is one of the bedtime prayers taught to children in the English-speaking Christian world when I was a child. Well, once you'd got into English. Where I was born, when you were just learning to pray — because you were now learning to talk and therefore compelled by the custom of the day to deliver your petitions to the heavenly father personally — your earliest solicitation in a German-speaking household might well have been: *Aber, Lieber Vater! Amen.* Delivered, even once you were past the halting lisping stage as: *Abba . . . Lieba . . .*

ah... um... *Fahta-amen!* And meaning — roughly: Now, for Pete's sake, God!

For most of this past winter the Four Angel Guardians prayer had been drifting through my head. While I was sawing wood. For the cook stove. Yes, I do have a SaskPower one, but SaskPower — or what *used* to be SaskPower before the Name-Changing Virus hit Saskatchewan governments — has this objectionable habit of sending you a letter requiring money off you every month if you have used its power. In fact, sometimes even if you haven't used so much as a single surge out of one kilowatt of its power.

Because these sandy loam acres grow it without charge the wood is free. And so is the wood saw. It does not run off SaskPower power or even off the power from Esso or Shell or Co-op. I found it in a storage building on my place. It used to belong to Grampa Story. It has a nail instead of a bolt where the blade is joined to the wooden frame, but no one sends me a bill for using it and that makes me smile every time I even pass that old square-arch-framed wood saw, never mind cut with it. And I pass it often because it sits right by the door so I can grab it up fast when it seems to be time to go out and cut a little more wood for the wood stove. This stove will also suffer coal, of course, but coal is scarcer than diamonds nowadays and twice as expensive, and I don't believe in using the name if I can't have the long-burning game, and so I now own just a wood stove. Check in with me, though, if you happen to hear I have sold five thousand copies of this book; I betcha that stove and I, to say nothing of the coal merchants, will be smiling wide as a Cheshire Cat in that case.

Anyway, sawing away — on the south side of the house so as to catch any sun and avoid any wind the day might be presenting — I began this winter to take notice that this old prayer kept cropping up.

Finally I began to listen to it. You can have a lot of stuff in your head and never listen to it. You can call that survival or you can call that missed opportunities, it all depends on your mind-set, but the way it is with me is, if you don't learn to listen to your own head, where are you? At the mercy of TV commercials and bank managers, to name two, that's where.

And when I listened I found out Mind was playing me a little joke. Because the prayer was being delivered like this:

*Matthew, Mark, Luke, and John*
*Guard the bed I lie upon;*
*Guard the pillow and the head,*
*And wake me up when I am dead.*

Well, well, well; an in-joke for reincarnationists!

Since I "got" it, I laughed. I am conditioned, by now, to jokes about reincarnation. I like to hear them. Most people who believe in it take it way too seriously, it seems to me. I mean, just because it's — well... a *principle,* they feel it has to be taken seriously. Like German Lutheran pastors of the Days of the Deep Dark Depression took the Theory of Transubstantiation. One of the smart alecs (male) in catechism class laughed at that one and sure enough he paid a price for it: he never made more than a quarter of a million dollars as long as he farmed and he lived only 80 years after his catechismic chortle.

I realize that, even this side of the Good Ship *Enterprise,* human beings have finally identified some of the basic principles of Spirit, just as they have identified some of the basic principles whereby the physical world operates. Those principles have been making the world (and us) go around since the origin of everything. The trouble is, it seems to me, the knowledge — even as far back as the ancientest of days — wound up in the hands of priests and shamans and scientists and economists, so the next thing we knew, we were in trouble.

Because they put their version of the way things really are in books and taught it to captive audiences, the younger the better. And they said, in effect, "If you try to experience the principles by yourself you will be burned at the stake or at the next world-wide Medical Specialists' Symposium; so listen up and toe the line, or else!"

I do sometimes read books about the physical principles, but they don't seem to stay in my head. I read books about the spiritual principles too, and the same thing happens. Unless there is something so basic, so non-negotiable, that I have somehow known it all along without knowing I knew it.

And that's the way it was with me and reincarnation.

It is a scary word for a very simple and wonder-filled principle. Namely: the human mind-spirit essence can never die.

We can't say the same for the body, unfortunately. Or fortunately, depending on how you look at its pains and its pleasures. That "dust to dust" stuff definitely applies to that part of us called the body. And just as well, in my estimation, because, after so many decades of chemicals Mother Earth is in need, nowadays, of a little more organic fertilizer.

Here's the beauty of it: once you have been put through the mill — by a too-challenging life, by a Doubting Thomas mind, by a determined soul that is not at all above grabbing you by the short hairs and adding to your misery when the chips are down if it will teach you something — when you have utterly succumbed and don't care any more what the hell the truth *really* is, the knowingness steals in like a thief in the night and takes permanent possession of everything you ever were, and are, and ever will be.

And hey, once you *know* that what we call the personality or the consciousness is ever-ongoing, wow! you're right back in that cozy feather-ticked four-poster and guarded, even at Sixty Something, by angels.

Not necessarily Matthew, Mark, Luke and John. Not necessarily four, count 'em, four. But at least one. More often, one thousand.

Well, darn. All that reincarnation stuff isn't really part of this story. I'd worked — and fought and kicked and screamed — my way through ingrained disbelief long before I found Grampa Story's old wood saw hanging on a stout nail in the basement of a storage building on my place; long before I came back to this little old house to live again (Dare I say, to be born again?) amongst the maple and poplar and willow, within the space of coyotes and deer and bush rabbits. Within the space, too, of porcupines and box elder beetles, and the occasional skunk, but what the heck!

This story is, to make no bones about it, about my first conscious awareness of angels.

*Guard the pillow and the head,*
*And wake me up when I am dead!*

I kept sawing. At that time, in typical disciplined Saskatchewanian fashion, I used to allot myself so much time each day to saw wood. Thirty below notwithstanding; thirty other items on the agenda notwithstanding. I made myself get out there and saw wood for thirty minutes by the clock. So there would be some wood sawed, see, if it got forty below some day. When it got to *forty* below, of course, I sawed anyway, dashing into the house after every few chunks to dance a tarantella on the snow-catcher rug just inside the door in order to snap the blood into circulation. I sawed in order to have wood in case I got the 'flu and couldn't get out. I had too healthy a body to simply pray I would reincarnate again quickly overnight into a nice warm body in nice warm South Africa.

One day it was forty below and I had the 'flu, to boot. So of course I went out and sawed wood to prove to myself I wasn't really dying.

All that sawing of wood isn't really part of the story, either. Or maybe it is. Because, it seems, one of the ways to get an angel into your head, wanted or not, is to be engaged in something rhythmic. Aerobics is good; skipping, too. Walking is dandy. Those with sensual minds have supplied another example, I'm sure, as soon as they read the word *rhythmic*. But singing is another way, a much-prized one, once you get into this stuff — so long as you are loose enough not to insist on the original lyrics.

It happens in your head all the time, you're just not listening. For example:

> *Come to me, my melancholy baby,*
> *Cuddle up and don't you fry*
> *Eggs again today; the doctor ordered*
> *That you change your tune soon. By the way*
> *Did I tell you that*

. . . well, long before the fifth line, if it's the first few times you've been visited in song by your personal guardian angel, your surprise will have shut off the worded part of the communication. Maybe even the music, if you were really shocked.

So, as I was saying, I thought a head that delivered me jokes about reincarnation was pretty funny, so I laughed. But kept sawing. You need to concentrate on your cut if you are Virgoan and therefore must have your wood chunks sliced neatly and precisely with the ends nice. Like the bread you slice from a large round homemade loaf bread — each flat side on a 180 degree plane, not lop-sided and odd-angled and needing more peanut butter on one end than on the other. This literary peanut butter, it is clear, I hope, is being spread not on poplar or birch or maple, but on nice dark five-grain or vitamin-enriched white.

Anyway, I kept sawing. And as I kept sawing the prayer came back. So I smiled. But when it came around again to the *wake me up when I am dead* part, I stopped. How did that prayer *really* go? I stopped and searched my mind and as usual there wasn't a darn thing there so I wondered if I should go inside and phone the library or something.

*I'll* tell you, said the visitor-in-the-head.

"Who are you?" Those of you who say that you talk to yourself recognize this process, right?

I am John.

"Ya, sure. And is it Matthew, Mark, or Luke gets the next shift?"

*I am John!*

Well, what the heck. I've had some pretty peculiar experiences-of-the-mind the last ten years or so. And I've discovered, if you have a somewhat experimental nature and are no longer afraid of anything since having learned the penalty for sincerity is *not* to be hanged by the neck until dead, why, you can learn a lot from life on Planet Earth — to say nothing about life in other universes — from right inside your own head.

So I said, "What do you want, John?"

I want to help you.

"How are you at sawing wood?"

It's been fun so far.

Surprise. "But . . . ?"

But now I will show you something else. Saw, please.

I did. It was cold anyway and not to saw was dangerous. Nothing happened. So gradually I quit concentrating on John and the snippets of words that would form and be cut off, form and be cut off. Attention drifted. Other things — images, unformed thoughts, worn-out scenarios — sifted, drifted, through Mind and passed on.

And then . . . where does one find the words to describe it? . . . it was as though there were suddenly and at once two worlds, side by side, and I was in both. In the one world I was standing at rest beside the rather pitiful saw-horse I had built when I first moved out here to the country; I was looking at the maple tree that had flourished handsomely at the southwest corner of this little house in the nearly thirty years I have lived somewhere else; I remember feeling (no, not *thinking)* how beautiful that tree was and how joyful it was for me to share the place where it had chosen to place its roots.

In the second world, I was there and yet I was not there; but when I was there I was observing myself being myself beside the rickety saw-horse.

There were no words, only an idea: THIS IS WHAT IT IS LIKE TO BE AN ANGEL.

You have heard people say, "I can't really describe it, but . . ." And then they begin — stumbling over the words and stopping them and then tripping over the words that want to follow — to try to put into words something for which there are no words: a feeling; a dream without pictures in it; an experience of utter peace and connectedness that happened, perhaps, out in a fishing boat on a mirror-calm lake or when alone in the deep woods or standing with one beloved under the stars at night.

Words won't do for the telling. Language is an artificial tool, an invention of humankind, an attempt to communicate with others of one's own species so that we can in some measure cope with the experiment we are caught up in on this little planet.

So, I can't really describe it, either. A poet once told me of sitting quietly, contemplatively, among the hills of south Saskatchewan one sun-filled afternoon when all at once she found herself peering directly into the eyes of a red fox. "I can't really describe what happened, then," she said, "but for just a little while I was the fox and the fox was me, and we both knew it."

"And we *both* knew it!"

Connectedness. Maybe that comes close to it. A coming-together on the cobwebbed interfacing of the world of electric Spirit and the plane of the physical, perhaps.

It is easier to say we have been visited by angels. They are the connectors, the angel John tells me. They are the loyal and loving and adventurous essences of loyal and loving and adventurous people who once made poems or farmed farms or fought unnecessary wars when they were within the human form on this interesting little learning-place called Earth.

Maybe some of them cut firewood with a smooth-cutting saw before the days of SaskPower and cannot get it out of the system, he suggests, and so they learn to ride the mind-waves to make jokes within the head of a sixty-year-old woman who is just beginning to learn her connectedness with angels and with trees.

How to saw wood with an angel? Joyously. With time out for a few laughs.

# Falling into Winter

I once heard a wistful man say, late August, "The crows are bunching; winter's almost here." And I agreed, because it was kinder to do so than to say, "Whatever in the world are you talking about, winter is a *long* way away!" That night it snowed.

Winter begins with fall, of course. When I was younger and in love with words my own family never used, I most often called fall *autumn,* but now that I am older and want the comfort of old things and old ways I have gone back to talking about *fall* and leaving *autumn* to the poets.

I heard a lovely thing the other day. I heard that one of the societies among the Original Peoples of this part of the North American continent used to call the month of September the Moon of the Yellow Leaf.

Now isn't that beautiful? And accurate, too, except for the snowy surprise it sometimes gives us during an oddball kind of year. September *is* yellow. And gold and orange and amber and ochre and saffron and topaz and flaxen and Jersey cream and straw and buff.

I feel a poetic mood coming on, and if you are a one who does not care for poetic moods or poets, look out. September does that to me; it makes for poetic moods and poetic words and poetic feelings, and I love it.

September does that to me and so I carry it along in my heart and in my mind always into October, which does not have a whole lot going for it, in my estimation, given its Saskatchewanian propensity for too-early snows. It hardly has a thing going for it except early pilgrims, who really don't belong to me and my own people, and present-day pumpkin pie which I am soundly enamored of, providing the cook goes easy on the spices.

I was born in September. And September was busy on the farm in those days, and the day I was born the harvest wasn't done for the year as yet and my mother was rushed right off her feet.

(Into her bedchamber.)

She gave me a name that means "the fighting spear maiden," maybe because I fought so hard to be born in the Month of the Yellow Leaf that I had no consideration for my mother or for the harvest. My mother, I am sure, would rather have been actively employed in her kitchen feeding threshers than laid up with a new baby — and a *third* daughter, into the bad bargain — and devising ways and means to scare up enough money to pay a hired girl.

But anyway, as soon as ever I knew enough to enjoy anything I loved September and the days of harvest: the threshing and gleaning and the bringing in of garden stuff. That was worlds better than weeding potatoes or herding cows — and it tasted better too. Every hill of potatoes was a goldmine of surprises and you kept score to see if the reds or the whites produced more potatoes to the hill. And in a pocket of your overalls was secreted a twist of paper with salt in it, to snack on the small marbly ones rubbed clean of garden dirt on the knee of your denims.

Even nowadays, if I don't get the potatoes up by the first of October I feel I am letting somebody down.

Some securely programmed Adult Inside, no doubt. The Child Inside, even to this day, if I must be honest about it, would rather skip through yellow aspen poplar leaves on the way to the potato patch than dig for treasure when she gets there; the Child Inside calls the leaves gold coins and tries to leave them where they have fallen

among the dried vines; the Child Inside wants to
smell the damp smell of good black earth and of
yellow leaves carrying with them the hint of ripe
wheat and of earthy potatoes.

   When I was young and it was late September

      The Month of the Yellow Leaf
      I felt no sadness in me
      to see the leaves fly by on a sun-warm wind
      heavy with the smell of wheat
       promises
      given in July when things were green
      and cows were herded along a road
      allowance
      (the pastures being saved
      for horses, who refused to be herded
      — or, sometimes, even heard).

      When I was young and it was late, late
      into The Month of the Yellow Leaf
      I skipped to school laughing
      to see the cows in pasture with Papa's horses
      barbed wire their new keeper
      me skipping free and laughing
      through the gold of the yellow leaf.

I warned you we might get some waxing of the poetic here, didn't I? Well, forewarned is forearmed, as the teacher used to say when wanting to signal what we'd better be studying for the final Science exam. So if you're still with us, thanks. And breathe easy; next comes October and I, for one, am not too liable to wax poetic about that.

There's this about it, though: there's nothing like a rather cold, cloudy, windy day in October to set you to counting your blessings, if you've got any.

And if you don't watch the late news much to see how much better off you are than 90 percent of the rest of the world, there are times, I expect, when you're pretty sure you don't have any. Blessings.

If you do watch the news, sometimes your blessings are counted in negatives, anyway:

— Thank God I do not live in a refugee camp.
— Praise Allah I was not shot at today.
— By intercession of Lord Buddha I did not starve to death this year.
— *Et cetera.*

That's pretty depressing stuff, until you discipline the self to word it in a positive way:

— Thank God I live in a pretty safe part of the world with a pretty sound roof over my head.

(I tend to qualify the soundness of roofs whenever they become the subject of words because there is generally at least one on the place that is less sound than I wish it to be.)

— Praise Allah I can see and taste and walk and touch and feel and breathe (so long as the pollen season has gone the way of a high wind) a safe good lifestyle.

— By intercession of Lord Buddha (and a largely vegetarian diet) I have learned to make a dollar do almost what it used to (so long as I keep up constant guard) towards feeding three kids and a dog and a cat.

It seems somehow necessary to report here now that I myself have only two kids (who haven't been kids for quite a while now); that I no longer keep a dog; that I would never keep house for a cat even if Queen Elizabeth of Saskatchewan herself asked me to do so. I wouldn't want you to suppose I am offering examples from my own personal life here — even St. Francis of Assisi didn't always do that.

As far as the prayers go, though, I don't mind confessing that I don't care whom I call upon when in the need of some fast action, and am not above raising a hue and cry to wake God and Allah and the Lord Buddha all at the same time in case one or the other is a bit slow to swing into high gear on my behalf.

Oh yes. Counting the positive blessings. On a cold and windy October day when the corn stalks you've not had time to clear from the garden are whipping in the wind outside your kitchen window; when the pine trees, heavy with new cones, are bent almost double with the wind though they're so large SaskPower shows its authoritative self uninvited onto your place every two years or so to lop off their heads; when the wind blows that hard and it is cold enough to startle Jack Frost himself but you are safe and warm inside courtesy of SaskPower and your own industriousness which has paid the power bill, then, oh then, you think about your father who had to go out in October or January or unforgiving March to work for hours at a stretch in the cold and the wind.

The father who told you once, not too long before the cancer took him, that he really began to appreciate Saskatchewan as soon as he retired and could admire it from behind a kitchen window, winters, and not have to so much as stick his nose out the door supposing the wind howled for even seven days hand-running.

One of the prime blessings of my life nowadays, firmly past sixty and surer of things than once I was, is that I can send him a cheery hallo via the messenger of mind, whether he's taken spiritual wing to Bermuda to bask in the earthly sun again or is hanging loose in Dimension 7, which some people call the first heaven.

"Winter," I can hear some reader say right about now, "sure has a way of bringing out the weirdness of some Saskatchewanians!"

You bet! And if you think the foregoing was as weird as it gets, you should spend a winter in the Yukon and hear perfectly ordinary, sane people talking conversationally to the local gaggle of ravens whenever they (the people) step outside the door!

Not only that, but then this lawyer or this school teacher will turn to you and say, "The raven says things won't go so well today, but hang in, it will all come out in the wash."

It seems we have spun ourselves a fair weird distance from the subject of September? Well, maybe, until we remember that these weird raven-speakers are dwelling in that land to the north that is still ruled, at its very essence, by the principles of Mother Earth. And one of those principles is that everything speaks to everything, always, so it is hardly even a minor miracle when ravens speak and humans have learned to listen not only to ravens but to stones and to the gold hidden deep in some gully. Have learned to listen each day of life to them, not only in the Month of the Yellow Leaf.

# Moose Jaw, and Jitneys, and the *Saturday Evening Post*

Nearly fifty years ago, in my hopeful but ignorant youth, I once wrote a story in which a strong, blond, silent and ruggedly handsome Swede living on a farm in southern Saskatchewan enveloped a vaguely unwilling hired girl in his huge hairy arms. I had him wearing a buffalo coat at the time, one given to him by a Mountie whose life he'd saved in a beer parlour brawl.

My Swede bundled the girl and her half-hearted protests into his jitney and drove her to Moose Jaw over crisp, diamond-studded acres of snow to the tune of brass harness bells (which were to symbolize wedding bells, I suppose, if I was clued into such things back in those old "learn to do by doing" days when there was no Writers Guild in Saskatchewan; no Summer School of the Arts; no such thing as "creative writing" in the schools, for that matter).

I sent the story — I remind you I was youthful and hopeful and utterly ignorant — to the *Saturday Evening Post*. They didn't buy it, of course, but I got a very nice letter back from some editor asking: 1) What is Saskatchewan; 2) What or where is this Moose Jaw; 3) Whatever in the world is a jitney?

So I drew the guy a picture of a jitney, labelling the parts; then I thought I'd send him a dictionary definition of the thing as my artistic talents were pretty well nil, as they are, indeed, to this day. Well, I looked in every dictionary I could lay my hands on, including the teacher's — she was fresh out of Normal School and her books were all new and lovely, not wracked and chawed and pinioned as were most of the books in our little country school.

But her lovely new dictionary did not have a definition of 'jitney'; I pored over that book for a long time but I could not find it.

Nowadays I can. My "Canadian" *Funk & Wagnalls* says it is an American word meaning a motor vehicle which carries paying passengers, or else a small coin such as a nickel.

Well I don't care, when I was a kid, the jitney on our farm didn't cost any money to ride in, not even one red copper, let alone an American nickel. Our jitney was the little sleigh our dad liked to use to go to town in when the snow was deep and the horses would wear out in 12 miles or so hauling the bob-sleigh. The jitney was the sleigh my mother said she wouldn't be caught dead in — or dead under — because it was so tippy.

It was an open sleigh. It was built on the short front runners of a double-runnered wagon box-sleigh; if you were a real handyman the box came off and got stored beside the oat stack in the feedyard when you wanted to haul poplar poles on the runners alone, touring back and forth to some ravine for your firewood.

Our dad once snapped his ankle when such a load shifted. It threw him right off but he climbed back on again while it was still numb and I can still taste the fear of "something gone wrong again" when I replay that scene and hear him calling out to those of us who had gone out on the porch to greet him, "Call Ma, I've broke my leg, she'll have to take over." I think that was the story of our efficient mother's life: having to take over.

But that's not this story. Because a jitney sleigh was so short, so sawed-off, riding in it for any distance over drifted roads or fields after a good stiff erratic blow was like riding a choppy lake in a five-foot boat — very conducive to losing your morning porridge.

The jitney, mind you, is not to be confused with the jumper or caboose.

Those were closed-in rigs equipped with tiny — often homemade — tin heaters. They were also squat. They were also tippy. They were also nauseating. But they were rarely built on the wide heavy front sleigh-box runners as the jitney was. They had more slender cutter runners and many a closed-in caboose in the Saskatchewan of my childhood had begun life as a sporty open cutter somewhere in Ontario or Minnesota or Ohio.

They were even tippier than our open jitney, according to Mother. She said it was a wonder half the people who rode in them weren't burned to death when the heater coals spilled out along with the passengers going down a steep ravine.

One of the neighbors told her, "Shoot, it's generally so danged cold going to town in those things you can't heat a fire up hot enough to warm so much as spit over the flames."

As soon as ever you opened the caboose door to the winter elements, this uncle claimed, the darned fire froze to death. But then, this neighbor, being a hidebound bachelor, always rode a horse bareback to keep warm wherever he went in winter and I don't suppose he ever owned a caboose or a jumper or even a jitney.

I asked him about that once and he said yes, that was true, and he "never felt deprived about it, neither!"

Nearly fifty years ago, the man from the *Saturday Evening Post* wrote back and said thanks very much, the subject was quite fascinating and he'd seen snow a few times himself and had even ridden in a sled once, many kind regards.

There was no cheque enclosed.

Nowadays the *Saturday Evening Post* has gone the way of the dodo and of many other fine magazines and periodicals we once considered we would just as soon not live without. There have been so many changes in our day-by-day world that books have been written and sermons preached and seminars mounted to try to help us deal with the stress on body, mind and spirit caused by all those changes. So sometimes we find ourselves yearning for things that never change, casting about for something permanent, something that is dependably the same, comfortingly familiar.

I suppose memories come close to filling that need. I was never one to live in the past, perhaps because mine tends to have been fairly mundane, as pasts go. Anyway, I've found I can't afford to spend a lot of time reliving the good old days; it takes each day's energy just to keep up with the surprises the winds of change keep blowing in: a new way to bank your pension; a new way to pay your credit card bills; a new "recycled" look to your groceries, your cleaning products, your phone bill — I hear maybe even your car, next.

And if you can't keep up — and at least fairly cheerfully, at that — you might as well throw in the towel, the new "how to cope" books tell us.

So I keep plodding along day by day and I pretend that I am cheerful and that I am changing. Why, I even went to live for a year in Moose Jaw. No one was driving a jitney, but there was considerable tipping of other people's bob-sleighs going on in city council the whole year that I was there. It had to do with whether to build a public library or wait for a while (I seem to remember the year 2033 came up once or twice) because there was currently only about twenty million in the capital works fund.

Man alive, was I green as grass or what, nearly fifty years ago when I was grasping at the straw of rugged virile Swedes and barely willing maidens as the stuff of Saskatchewan drama!

I had a wonderful time the year I lived in that tippy city where Al Capone and his cronies once hung out — though not, I gather, at weekly council meetings. And one night after a decision on the new library had been postponed yet again, I was lying in this fine old Murphy bed in this clean little bachelor pad in an old apartment building over a flower shop. And without warning the memory of the *Saturday Evening Post* breezed in. And I forgot all about the archaic working conditions in the glorious Moose Jaw heritage library. And for a while again I was happy.

Which is, to me, a demonstration of how I've accepted the discipline of change, let me tell you. Even five years ago I'd have felt compelled to mount a campaign, run for mayor, and try to build that new Moose Jaw library myself.

# Northward, Ho!

It took me over fifty years to get my first glimpse of Canada's north country after having dreamed igloos and Eskimaux (we used to say Eskimos) when I was a kid and going to a little country school in the droughty, good old, bad old days. Back in the time when you wished, some years, that you could order in snow from Eaton's so there'd be sure to be enough for Christmas — and for the business of being an Eskimo because we'd been studying them again in school.

When the Eskimo fever was upon me it was hard to have to round up snow in the wheelbarrow to get enough to make even a pretend igloo that had no "inside." If it had no inside what point was there in trying to make — and, of course, to light — a seal-blubber oil lamp out of a sneaked saucer, some paraffin wax from the supplies in the jelly-making cupboard, and a chunk of store string — of which there was so much around, even in those impoverished times, that people had great balls of it wound up and stored in a junk drawer in the pantry.

Fifty years after the fact, give or take a few years, I finally saw the True North, strong and still relatively free, at least of tourists. It took me six years, after that, to get back there again, for the Call of the North — though often as strong and compelling as Nelson Eddy pretending to be a Canadian Mountie and giving a melodious *Yoohoo!* for Jeannette MacDonald against a backdrop of pine forest and mountains — was all too often over-ridden by the strident voice of one's budget when it came to anything beyond the monthly bills and a little healthcare insurance.

Anyway, finally I got to go back and I had to travel light, because I was not going this time via the back passenger seat in a family-owned four-wheel-drive, as I had the first time, but by way of an airline company — pick and choose a name, it seems to me they are all fond of losing one's luggage even in as short a booster lift as from Saskatoon to Regina.

Travelling light, thank goodness, gets easier as you get older and have finally received the ultimate enlightenment: the one who packs it at home is the one who has to pack it on the road. And not just as far as the airline counter. If you and your luggage have the good fortune to meet again at the other end of your flight you will likely be obliged to further the bonding process up several sets of stairs from the baggage carousel, and out to a cab, and up and into the luggage compartment of said vehicle. (Item #127 of the Cabbies' Manifesto states that under pain of death will a driver even get out from behind the wheel to *assess* the weight of a bag, let alone lift it. Item #126 lays out the penalties for getting out from behind the wheel to open a door for the paying passenger.)

If you are the one who has packed it into a travel bag nowadays you are also likely to be the one who gets to carry it up hill and down dale, so to speak, at railway stations and hotels — except for the chains who pretend to "old-fashioned service." That actually means a disinterested male anywhere between the ages of sixteen and eighty-seven and dressed like a toy-box soldier or a grenadier guard, who will slap your bags on a dolly along with those of eighteen other people, and bring them to your room three hours later, one hand already out — and it doesn't do, I've learned, to mistake it for a good old-fashioned *welcome* handshake. That is, they will deliver the bags three hours after you have, in travel-weary desperation, had a shower, washed your smalls at the sink, and wrapped your body in a bedsheet to await, in the good old-fashioned way, with weary patience whatever you need in your baggage.

The foregoing has been largely an unpaid editorial comment, so to speak, from The Inner One, who has had it up to here with being spiritually forgiving about airlines and cab companies and so has degraded Herself sufficiently to pass the word down to me, the long-suffering Lutheran non-complainer. When it comes to this Inner One, believe me, I have to do what I'm told ever since having made a Thy-will-be-done agreement with this self-same Inner One somewhere along the way.

This Inner One is sometimes called The Higher One in books drawn from the self-improvement section of your local library. And this Inner One/Higher One we are beset by, as many besides myself have discovered, can be just as snarky as the poor little downgraded physical one of us when it finds itself compelled to wear the same travel outfit for a week while the airline pretends to be tracking down the lost duffel bag; in fact, I have known one such Inner One/Higher One just as good at cutthroat cussing as any poor mortal, when a cab driver has made far too many circlings in our own neighborhood to get us to our own front door "the short way" from the airport.

I expect there's been at least one reader by now who has turned back to the first page at least three times to check the title, said, "Yep. It *says* Northward, Ho! all right," and scratched the head in bemusement. Well, this is so going to be a story about going to the North, I promise you. It's just that sometimes these little forays down Snark Alley seem to be required of me by The Inner One — who frequently tries to pass herself off as The Higher One, but who is likely really nothing more than The (Unholy) Writer Inside.

I just have to put up with these things, for Herself controls (supplies, or dries up) the words that come down the mind's silver channel and is therefore to be humoured more often than not.

So that's settled.

Now. This second time that I travelled to Canada's True North strong and free it was not July and raining cats and dogs and assorted fishes as it had been the first time that I went. It was raining *rain,* by the jiggies, as though all the prayers of droughted Saskatchewan were to be answered by a flood that was required, for some cosmic reason, to begin at Fort St. John.

We didn't get off at Fort St. John, my travel companion and I. We said if it was going to rain like that we would stay put and grow fins first. But the truth is, we weren't booked in for Fort St. John, we were bound for Whitehorse. And there, rain or no, we would be turfed out into the hands of a welcoming committee promised us by phone and by letter.

It was National Book Festival Week in Canada and, along with a Saskatchewan poet of proven good cheer and high repute, I had been invited to instill a few writing techniques and a lot of inspiration into some high school students in Whitehorse, Yukon Territory.

That's why there was a welcoming committee. It was a working trip and in our particular business it is the business of those who have invited you to lay on the added bonus of being met at the airport by smiling people who are purportedly delighted to meet you; who have, moreover, a car out front, rather than a cab, to take you to your hotel; who will, never fear, *insist* on not only lifting your bag but also carrying it as soon as and whenever needed the whole time they are with you, and who, when they hold out a hand to you, will be intending for you to shake it.

If you have never experienced a Northern welcome, you have something to look forward to. Once you have, you have something to write home about. In this case, our welcomer was so delighted to see us and so interested in looking after us graciously that he forgot another body from the East was coming in on the same plane, and we left that Ontario chappie at the airport. The Inner One, I am happy to report, did *not* say, "Oh well, it's only an Easterner!"

So OK. The theme of this piece is: Northerners, on the whole, really *are* hospitable and kindly-intentioned, and ready-to-take-everything-in-stride "great folks": it is not just Tourism hoke.

Talk about old-fashioned welcomes! Why, all of us weren't even in the door yet, when the woman behind the hotel reception desk — with a telephone apparently glued to her ear, for she used both her hands to do other things all the while she was talking — called out to us, "Hello, hell-*lo! Welcome* to the Yukon, what do you mean there's no lock on your door? . . . oh I see, there's no *door* there."

Remodelling was going on, she told us, but the several rooms of the visiting writers (i.e. — Hurray! — us) *had* been fitted, she assured us, with locks. (Which meant, one hoped, that they'd been fitted with doors, too.) And if not, she went on, phone still crazy-glued to one ear, report it at once please and it would be seen to quicker than you could say Jack Robinson. I'm pretty sure she really said Jack *London,* but I'm not going to put that down here for who would believe it anyway, I ask you?

Our welcomers, after we had wrestled our bags from them at the elevator in a fit of prairie independence, urged us to take tea at the Yukon's expense as soon as we cared to in the hotel's restaurant — which was *not* outfitted with 157 varieties of gold pans and old shovels and other rickety-rackety old mementoes to celebrate the Bad Old Days as is the current mode of eateries along the tourist trail in the prairie west where old buggy wheels and coal-oil lanterns and re-finished flat irons grace old barn-lumber walls, thereby causing old "pioneers" like my mother, who have had to use the darn things, gag at their soup-of-the-day.

Furthermore, urged our Yukon welcomers, please meet them for something a bit stronger than tea, and for dinner after that, a bit later on; and leave your wallet in your room, they said, they didn't take Saskatchewan money up here in the Yukon.

Well now, it seems I have just backed myself into a corner here. And it is just as awkward — maybe more so — to get painted in by words than by urethane black walnut varnish.

I have got painted in because, back a ways, I got sucked into believing it was The Writer Inside who was telling me the theme of this piece. Now I see it was only the dismal little computer called mind that was doing it — the practical, I-need-to-know Left-Hand Mind.

When you have been writing all day you get to worry about how it's going; it's harder to hear the words as they come down the silver channel and so you start demanding that you want to know things.

Sitting at the long kitchen table with the new-fangled plastic cover that looks like good sturdy old-fashioned oilcloth but isn't, I somehow had the good sense to be quiet for a while and let the busy chatty mind quit intruding the sensible thing, the obvious.

And The Writer Inside sneaked in like a boxer after the first feint or two and clobbered me with the message: It has nothing to do with Northerners, silly; it has to do with the North itself.

Well, immediately you argue. I mean, there's this Yin and Yang thing to uphold, right? So, "Surely not so!" you say to The Writer Inside. "Surely the North *land* is downright *in*hospitable. All that ice and snow! All that need for cremation in order to thaw out enough on the trail so you can be glad to be there! Surely it's the *people* who make the North what it is, and make you so glad you got to go and to be there."

But here's the rest of the story. Along with the parties and the invigorating sessions with talented and courteous students, along with the political figures (who feel writers and their writing are not only important, but essential to the way of life of the Yukon), along with the conducted tours and the casual drives to overpowering views of the landscape, the hospitable Yukoners gave you time to be alone with the Yukon.

I didn't say *in;* I said *with*. Time to be alone *with* the Yukon.

I walked along the river and I listened to the conversation of mind, and I was given the blessing of knowing *within* that there are consciousnesses/personalities/spirits who will never leave the Yukon. Their energy-essences have been — by some cosmic chemistry I cannot explain but can no longer doubt — so irreversibly subsumed by the life-energy of that immense and once utterly pure land, that they will live there, adding to that zapping Yukon energy, half-way into forever or as long as there is a Yukon alive on this planet.

One of those mind-presences who visited me said: Come where I tell you to go, and I will show you a Yukon crocus today.

Well, part of the instructions were in words, but mostly it was just action. I was hustled like a robot along a busy highway; the rush and the noise were awful. I am never so in awe of mind-presences that I cannot express honest opinions and I remember "saying" that Yukon drivers are the wildest I've experienced since Main Street, Winnipeg, where I came close to being flattened like a paper doll at least twice a week the year that I lived in that city.

Then, all at once, I found the body sprinting, upon some sort of cue, across the road and off into the forest.

There I came upon a trail which obviously many had walked upon, perhaps also to escape the message of what whirling wheels and blue-grey exhaust were doing to the Yukon. And suddenly, there they were: the crocuses.

All the next day I reported, all over the place, those crocuses. One person said, "Oh, are they out already?" No one said, "Yes, I've seen them too." I shut up about crocuses.

Another day I was "given" to know that I must cross the river again and climb the hill near the hospital to the little cemetery one can see from the downtown side of the river. There were two tiny white "houses" there and two rectangles of white picket fences about the size of a single bed. The wooden crosses and headstones said things like "BIG SALMON JIM AND WIFE"; "JEWELRY HANSEN"; "ANNIE LIM"; "NETTIE ERECTED BY HER FRIENDS OF TESLIN."

There were more crocuses too, darker-hued than those of home and very lovely. There were gophers, three of them, standing ninety degrees erect, the sentinel posts for the apices of a perfect equilateral triangle.

There was a robin somewhere in the bush singing: Bring it here, please, Gertrude! over and over and over until I made acknowledgement that I understood what it was saying.

I could only suppose that the robin's *it* meant my butt, so I moved it; but when I walked into the bush towards the singing I couldn't seem to get any closer to the singer. I stopped. And I heard that practical Left-Hand Mind say: Go back now; how would they ever find you in this bush? You told no one where you were going!

I stayed on the path, at the behest of some sort of Mind-Guide, and almost back-tracked to the robin before it flew up and away very close to me and looking very sassy.

A long time after I was home again — back in a safe quiet little house on a safe quiet piece of prairie land that grows crocuses quietly in a sunny open patch in the bush that is technically "mine" now, I got one of those lovely "reinforcements" that Spirit presents when we have put Mind aside for the moment and are simply "being there." It happened because I had one of those inexplicable whims one gets at times, and to which I have learned to yield, now that I am past sixty.

I was not in the bush but in the house. The little inner nudge I received was to go quickly into the front room and turn on the television. I was working at the computer at the time and things were going OK, but I did as the whim, the nudge, bade, anyway.

The North was the subject. And soon, a woman of about my age was shown, speaking to this effect: It is my land and I need to be alone with it; I feel that I am the Yukon and the Yukon is me, and anyone else being there is not wanted and is not needed.

So there we are. The word we must use is hardly *hospitable*. *Necessary* seems to come closer to it. It has been often said and often recorded by those who have been granted "enlightenment," sometimes nowadays called "the peak experience," that there are *no* words adequate to even begin to report such a happening to anyone else.

When a joke falls lame, we say, "I guess you had to be there."

That's it. *You* have to be there. Whether you want to know the fascinating and beautiful and sometimes threatening North land of the spirit or the fascinating and beautiful and sometimes threatening North land of Canada, you have to go there, be there. If it hasn't happened to you, it hasn't happened. For it is a connection of sorts, and it is holy.

And when it has to do with the Yukon, if the Yukon is *necessary* for you, it is necessary for you to make that connection *alone!*

# Protesting the Protestant Work Ethic

I hate the Protestant Work Ethic. Even if I were as solidly non-Protestant as the Pope or the Buddha, I would hate the Protestant Work Ethic. At least I would, if I were free to hate anything anymore. But now that I have discovered that to allow yourself to hate anything is not good for your Inner Other, let me say instead that I am out of kilter with the Protestant Work Ethic and I just can't take it anymore.

It was bad enough when I was younger and had the energy to do the work that any Work Ethic worth its salt demands of those living under its jurisdiction, but the years are catching up to me and I can't run as fast as I used to.

There used to be an old saying: Never run if you can walk; never walk if you can sit; never sit if you can get comatose on the couch before somebody else gets there before you. (OK, that's a paraphrased version.) Needless to say, that old saw — or a version thereof — never got stitched into wall samplers, along with GOD BLESS OUR HOME, by those born into the Protestant Work Ethic. Who had time to sit and sew wall samplers when there was a hamper full of holey socks to be darned and Auntie Margaret's last year's coat to be made down for young Lucy for the coming winter?

I know that an awful lot of people in this world work hard and thrive on it; they wouldn't think to complain of it even to their mothers, while to sit still for half a day to put the words of complaint on paper would be to them an utter waste of time — and would keep them away from pouring a yardful of cement or steaming the wall paper joyfully from junior's bedroom or chasing a hundred flighty cows, for lack of anything else to do, down a dusty trail to the back pastures. My whole trouble is, I was born lazy — I would like to say "as lazy as a pet 'coon" because I heard a pretend cowboy say that once in an American movie and was quite taken with it, but from what I've learned about Canadian racoons they are not too lazy to get into everything they can find, if left alone in the house. In fact, so I've heard, they tend to investigate it all so busily that it costs a year's salary to doctor up the damage and even at that you are finding teeth and claw marks in the most surprising places three years after they've gone to the happy chewing ground of a local zoo.

When you have been born as lazy as a doorstep in the hot summer sun, it's just too hard to live up to the energy draining Protestant Work Ethic and that is that.

You take, when I was a kid, utterly foreign to Planet Earth and prepared to live here at all, in those dry and hot and dusty days, only if I could live in books, I was set to herding cows. Because I was useless anyplace else. I was always plumping down somewhere to read the book I had smuggled along in my jersey. So I suppose my dad figured I might as well be far enough away from the frustration threshold of my efficiently hardworking older sisters and so at least keep a little aggravation at bay.

I always took a book along. Boldly. Not hidden. My dad didn't like the idea but my mother always let me take along *King Arthur* or *Anne of Green Gables*. My dad said, in his own way, that Tinker made a better companion. He didn't mean Tinker Bell either, he meant Tinker the dog. And don't kid yourself, there'd be work involved for Tinker too: he would have to help keep the cows out of Uncle Bill's green oats when I was set to herd those black and white mulching machines along the herd allowance.

And I'd no sooner have climbed up in the Camelot Tower of my favourite black poplar, it seemed, when Tinker would bark away off to hell and gone from Camelot. And sure enough, when I came back into this world, there'd be the cows efficiently ignoring old Tinker who was making vicious soft-gummed forays at their heels in Uncle Bill's green oats. And I'd have to climb down the intricately laid-out secret steps of Camelot's watchtower and run to beat old *aitch*, trying to keep a desperate bobbing eye on Uncle Bill's place into the bargain to see if anyone was out and about and looking. Because they were still all mad at us over there from the last time it happened.

(From the last time I *let* it happen.)

And my heart would be pounding because I was not as good a runner as those cows but it was my job now to get fast fast fast to each and every Holstein and get them out of the green oats the only way they seemed to understand.

I'd pelt up to each one in turn and look her in the soft brown eyeball and I'd say, "You get the hell out of here fast or I'll tell my dad to sell you to the butcher next Cow Day." And they didn't seem to know I had about as much influence with my dad as did Sir Walter Scott or Mr. R.B. Bennett, both pretty low on the totem pole in his particular Protestant Work Ethic estimation, so those cows would turn tail and charge hell bent for election for the road allowance.

They all made separate trails, of course, through the conscientiously growing green oats, and left the field by as many new holes in the barbed wire fence as there were cows: those cows knew a thing or two about the Work Ethic and didn't mind putting themselves out at all for it.

On my behalf. For I'd then have to work furiously, trying to prop posts up if they still had their feet close enough to the ground to get propped, and trying to find deadfall in the bush still strong enough to stand the strain of getting "woven" into the wires in the stretches where a post was broken and swinging from the top wire like a happy monkey doing a one-handed workout on a bar in a zoo.

And my muscles would freeze, and so would my heart, if I heard a rider come cloppety-clopping down the road, in case it was one of Uncle Bill's boys, or maybe even Uncle Bill himself, who wasn't a "real" uncle anyway so why was a man with a furiously dancing moustache even called that?

And I'd be tired, so tired. And I'd pass my hand in blessing, like the pastor on a Sunday, in the general direction of the cow trails in the green oats, and I'd say — within my head, of course, because the ears of oats didn't need it said aloud to them — "Now you grow back nice and green and even and *fast* before that Uncle Bill comes by or I'll pray for a frost to kill you tonight!" It might be ninety-two in the shade, but I was desperate. And, mind you, sometimes it worked.

If you're thinking to yourself, She didn't learn *that* out of *King Arthur,* I'm afraid you have forgotten about Merlin the Magician and Morgan le Fay and all that. I mean, it wasn't all courteous jousting and gallant bedding of the king's lady back in those romantic times, you can bet your boots on that.

And then, Morgan le Fay be praised, we moved to town and I still wanted only to live in Camelot and be a lady, but I had to scrub floors instead. Not for my mother, she did the floors in that good solid only-twenty-years-old "new" house gladly herself, or got my efficiently hardworking sisters to cheerfully do so when they were not doing a hundred other things.

No, I was scrubbing the floors of the mothers of the girls I went to school with, the jobs handed down to me, so to speak, when my older sisters "recommended" me when they themselves went on to work even harder at a café and drugstore. By the time I was in high school they announced they had held a job for me long enough and so the next thing I knew I was wearing a white smock and a clean white apron (which didn't stay clean beyond the first twenty minutes of any given day) and slapping hot hamburger sandwiches and chips in front of university students who sometimes said, "Are you *sure* you're a sister of the girl who never made us wait?" and so put me in the dungeon of some dark old place that didn't feel at all like Camelot.

And if you so much as slackened off, back in those days, and tried to steal a look at the daily paper, never mind the uncondensed version of *Morte d'Arthur* from the library, there was somebody who generally came by — an efficiently hardworking older somebody — to ask you if you would soon be ready to turn an honest living.

And so, and so, it was eventually my job to get married and I did. And wound up marking English and Math papers at the kitchen table in between scrubbing floors and baking bread and cleaning fish and soaking darkened venison in cold salted well water to make mincemeat so as not to waste the "shot" meat of a deer.

And then, and then, I reached a stage in my life when I had angel voices in my head, and one of the things they said to me was, "Sit down in the sun for the next twenty years and listen to the Mind telling you how to listen."

It sounded too tempting. That's how it is when you have been trapped by the Protestant Work Ethic almost before you got spilled from the cradle. You tell yourself that soothing angelic voice is really the devil in disguise. And, instead of learning how to listen to the Arthurian legend of your own personal and individualized mind, you go to university.

At the age of forty-seven, twenty-six years beyond the age of reason, you go into a Liberal Arts course, at that. And since I came out of it, four (or maybe forty) years later with a medal that's supposed to be worth two hundred dollars if you melt it down for its gold, I am not going to suggest some of the ways to make *un*liberal a student's time in a Canadian university. Even though that would work right in with the tenets of the Protestant Work Ethic, one of which decrees: Rules are rules, and it's always somebody else besides you who gets to set them.

Around about then, to my great blessing, the still small voice that lies secluded in each of us to save us from desperation roared loudly into my head with the following message: SOMETHING GOOD WILL COME OF ALL THIS!

And it did, too. For one thing, I lived through it.

That's the trouble with work ethics. If you live through the work you fool yourself into thinking it has made you smarter and stronger.

So when you are nearly sixty and your son says, "If you're going away to work for a year you'll need a place to store the stuff from your city apartment, so why don't you move it out to the farm?" you fall for it.

The people who last lived there have not scrubbed the walls as promised; the basement is soggy and likely harbouring spiders and toads, if not full-grown iguanas; the roof in the porch leaks and there is no plumbing. But you've been well-schooled by now.

"Oh I can do it," you say. "And when I come back from that contract job I will live here for a while and get my head settled."

And after you have scrubbed and painted for over a week and are so tired you would rather die than lift another finger, you drag yourself outside to the chokecherry bush that has blessed the front door here for fifty years and is now about as tired as you are. You have a pail of cold well water and are about to wash out the paint brushes.

And you say, to the Angel-devil who has brought you here on the wings of Oh-I-can-do-it, "It's bloody well nothing but work, work, work in this life; where is this Bluebird of Happiness people write songs about, is it only for the Buddhists and the Catholics?"

And flashflashflash there is a very blue and very alive bluebird before you, *and hovering* there, right in front of your very eyes.

And inside you the still small voice asks, very, very clearly: Is this close enough for you, Gertrude?

That evening, you sit outside, righteous as a nun, or at least a deaconess, because your house is now clean and in good order. All about you it is quiet. And a deer comes by. Having sailed over *your* fence it now picks its way unconcernedly past *your* maple trees and on into *your* alfalfa field, browsing as it goes, never lifting its head to check for dangers.

It trusts the place. It has worked it over, one might say, in its efficient version of the Work Ethic, and now it is taking its ease.

As I am.

Until the next job comes along.

I will take my chances with a better good will now, I trust, with the work that comes my way. At least it is not too liable to be the job of escaping a man with a loaded gun, a sometimes fulltime job for my new calm and quiet friends, the silently hardworking deer.

# The Sounds of Silence

Let this be about SOUND. We likely don't think about sound too much, unless our lives revolve around some form of it. Musicians, perhaps, think about sound a lot. Or perhaps they don't either: they just make it, experience it, live it.

Some of us become more concerned with sound when our solid, efficient hearing begins to falter; when we find ourselves having to ask people to repeat what they've said; when we don't quite catch the punch line of a joke because the storyteller "isn't as good as he used to be, he garbles his words a lot, doesn't he?" I'm slowly slipping into that category and there is nothing so disquieting as to have to ask a whole roomful of kindergarteners the name of one of their number because "this gramma didn't quite get it" after three repetitions by a wide-eyed and hefty-lunged charmer who finally gets really cheesed off with having to repeat his name.

I finally told The System of All Things I was going to quit working in the schools if things didn't improve. I threatened God, you might say. And I guess The System of All Things wanted me to keep on being a work-horse because things seemed to improve quite a bit after that and I haven't been having too much trouble in that department the last couple of years. The scientifically minded — i.e., left-brained — Reader will be saying here, "Aha! She learned to lip-read and doesn't even know it, but then, what can you expect of these flighty artist types!" The creatively minded — i.e., the right-brained types — may well speculate on the triumph of mind over matter, or of extra energy being pumped in by angels to help overcome a slight hearing loss. Either way is OK with me.

Anyway, the loss of the hearing is not what I meant to talk about here. It is more along the line of hearing too much, too well.

The easiest way to tell this is as a story. So. I was on my way home again. To my eighty-six acres of bush and sand near Saskatoon-the-sometimes-beautiful. I'd been gone for several days. It was growing dusk when I turned off what we call "the Biggar highway" onto the sandy road that was just a grassy trail thirty years ago when we first lived in that area, the sandy road that gets better and better to navigate the more it has rained.

It had just rained. The natural perfumes of green growing things assailed the nostrils, the inner recesses of mind. That was the first thing. Then, the stillness crept in. And as soon as I recognized it, yielded to it, expressed inner gratitude for it, it enveloped me, the car, the "city stuff" I'd been dragging along with me in the mind and body: it eased its way around me, enveloping me like a security blanket, a comfy, cool, just-warm-enough envelope of quiet, of calm, of lovely being-without-noise.

The sound of stillness is surely one of the blessings of life on Planet Earth. I for one can quite accept that Spirit first descended into flesh partly to get away from the too-much-sound of other galaxies, other dimensions. But by now we are as busily polluting this beautiful little blue and green experimental planet with noise as we are with PCB's and such.

(About PCB's. I always want to say *BVD*'s! I guess that shows my mind prefers to live back in "the good old days" — which weren't all that good, in many ways — when, after a long sweaty, sweary day of cutting wood in the bush, your

BVD's were pronounced as polluting the atmosphere of the hot kitchen and you were invited to take yourself out to the cow barn if you didn't mean to go change your underwear immediately.)

Anyway, during that particular "at home" time, about the only sounds I heard during the day were the sounds of the singing of birds and the chop of the axe while I finished clearing out a chokecherry bush near the house. Well, there was the sound of something else for a while, also familiar from the good old, bad old days, at least for a while — when a chunk of chokecherry whapped me just above the eye and blood spurted as from a newly released artesian well. I have lived a calm and relatively "pure" life for so long now that I am quite startled to discover the "blue" words suitable for such an occasion are still stored in the grey-mattered computer and, moreover, are immediately accessible. You don't have to hunt for them at all, at all!

The sounds I heard at night were these: the coyotes telling me I was too tired to go walking in the bush alone after midnight; the stars singing promises of life in other dimensions; the aurora zapping life-energy closer and closer as the nightside of life wore on. The occasional burrowing hum of a mosquito. The furry flutter-flutter of a moth. Grass growing. Maybe. An old neighbour in these parts once told me grass did most of its growing at night; he'd taken the trouble to measure it. Other neighbours said if that neighbor would only spend more time working in the fields and less time speculating and experimenting he'd be better off and his banker would be happier. And I didn't doubt those neighbours any more than I had doubted the grass measurer: I'm pretty easy when anybody tells me anything.

That's not quite all I heard, standing on the front step in the starshine/aurora dust, breathing in the essences of natural things and absorbing the sounds of a quiet night. Without warning, at two o'clock in the morning, "SHE-EE BAROKE MAH HEART!" whanged its way to me from god knows where beyond the bush.

A new acreage has been let, I suppose. I shall check it out this summer. If somebody means to barake my heart (and my silence) every night from now on I suppose I'd better check out the possiblities for peace and quiet in the hardly-populated Yukon.

Ah well. A "psychic artist" once drew a picture of me as an Eskimo. (Nowadays we say *Inuit,* but when she drew and coloured the picture she and

I and almost everybody else said *Eskimo,* so that's how I report it.) She said she had seen me in that way many times in dreams and in the silences she is given by her angels so that she can hear and see in that special way many know about now quite fearlessly. I'm pretty darn sure I wouldn't want to spend a Saskatchewan winter in an igloo, but I'm also pretty darn sure very few of The People, which is what *Inuit* means, do so anymore, either, in Canada's interesting North.

Whether one who wants a relatively unbaroken heart could actually live up there "on the pension" and a few dollars per annum of book royalties, depends on how much heating oil costs up there, maybe. Or what kind of a deal I can make with whoever keeps breaking faith with the sound of silence in the new acreage next to mine in that (fairly) quiet spot I own in my own dear homeland of Saskatchewan.

# Doing Co-operation

I am writing this in my office in a little old house set on eighty-six acres just west of Saskatoon. I lived in this small house once before, nearly thirty years ago. Then it was called a country school teacherage and I lived here with Joe Story who was then the teacher for the small A-frame-plus-a-squared-box stuccoed school.

When we moved here our children were a teething and generally distressed one-year-old and a mature little old lady just about ready for school. What is now my office was their bedroom; what is now the bathroom was a laundry room and "library." There was plenty of room for the four of us plus a patient old dog who joined us on nights when it was threatening thirty below: now there is hardly room for me and a computer and all the junk one person accumulates over thirty years of living — even living "on the move."

Yesterday my granddaughter came to stay the day. She is three and just lately in Pre-school. "It isn't *school*, yet, you know, Oma. It's only *pre-school*, you have to say it *pre-school,* see?" It was time for a mid-afternoon snack and to tell you the truth I was just about caved in and ready, like Winnie-the-Pooh, for a little something sweet and sticky, preferably a gooey donut with raisins and apples baked inside.

But when a modern child with careful parents is in your charge you offer (and help to eat) sliced red apple, some on each plate, and a communal bowl of shelled peanuts, set precisely half-way between the two of you at the kitchen table.

The kettle is singing on the wood stove. She munches apple, says, "I like the kettle singing."

"I like it a lot myself," you say. The apple is not doing the trick and your body is yelling for starch and sugar.

She reaches into the peanut bowl, transfers a small pink handful dribbling to her plate. "I'm putting some on my own plate," she says. "I love peanuts, they're good."

I resist the temptation to pontificate, "And they're so good for you, too!" Haven't I just heard on the late night news that the faithful, trusty, cheap, nourishing peanut is now guilty of carrying carcinogens? That being the case, the world might just as well do its second Big Bang bit and be done with it, in my opinion.

"I'm glad you like them," I say.

"I didn't take all of them, Oma."

"No, of course not, you're a sharer." She likely understands *sharer,* I told myself.

"If you take them all," she says, "then that's not doing co-operation, and if you don't do co-operation then people might not play with you at recess." Munch, crunch, smile; munch, crunch, smile. "Right, Oma?"

When I get my wits back I say, "Right!" Three years old — well OK, nearly four — and she's talking co-operation as casually and as appreciatively as she talks new book bag or a new tooth for baby brother.

I just love it, don't you, when your own belief system comes back to you across your own kitchen table? I have said for years and years that here in Saskatchewan we absorb Co-operation with a capital 'C' with our mother's milk or with our cow brand formula. No matter the political stripe of the parliamentary gang who at any given time is leading us to the shearing pens, the principle of Co-operation is safe in Saskatchewan and even a right-wing crew sitting in those cozy and ornate governmental chairs in the queen's Saskatchewan city would not dare to gainsay that principle openly.

Co-operation is as Saskatchewanian as Medicare and Good Old Prairie Hospitality and in spite of its age it seems to be alive and well and living a life of its own in our "doing co-operation" pre-schools.

# The Way Spring Springs to Mind

*Spring has sprung, the grass is riz,*
*I wonder where the birdies is;*
*They say the bird is on the wing:*
*How absurd! I always heard*
*That the wing was on the bird!*

In my salad days, versifiers and punsters like Ogden Nash were much given to making fun of old saws and cliché'd poetic phrases whether they were about Spring or about anything else they could put into their cheek along with a little tongue.

I used to be quite taken with the likes of Ogden Nash and Richard Armour and Robert Bentley and Dorothy Parker and a few more I might mention if I was still enamoured of such humour.

For some reason or other it seems to be apropos to mention that when I was a whole lot younger I found the Springy verse quoted above even funnier when it was presented in Brooklynese, to wit:

*Spring has sprung, da grass is riz,*
*I wonda wheah da boidies is.*
*Dey say da boid is on da wing, etc. etc.*

When we were laughing our heads off about that, none of my contemporaries — so far as I know — had ever been to Brooklyn. Most of us hadn't even been to Regina. Poor example. Most of us high schoolers in late 1940's Saskatoon had already picked up on the intense rivalry between the two major Saskatchewan cities and wouldn't have been "caught dead" in Regina "on a bet." As far as we were concerned, Reginans were weird people, perhaps even from another planet, though some of us had not so far met or talked to one.

We had never heard a bona fide Brooklynite speaking, either. All we knew about the way such fascinating foreigners talked was what we heard at the movies or on "The Life of Riley" and other comedy shows of that ilk on the radio.

I find it somewhat interesting (and maybe even a little bit depressing) that what springs so readily into mind when I think there's nothing going on in there is a thought or a memory that has its origins south of the border (and I don't mean Down Mexico Way, either). It's as though our

"Canadian" minds had been bought lock, stock, and barrel long before Free Trade and the killing of assistance to Canadian-made books and newspapers.

And maybe there is nothing necessarily wrong with that. Maybe designated countries are artificial and unnecessary and even downright dangerous. Maybe what is needed on this experimental planet is a way for those who live on the same *geography* of a continent to be bonded, or aligned, or working together as a community. If a south Saskatchewan Spring springs also upon those eagerly awaiting the end of Old Man Winter on the prairieland of Montana, maybe all those anticipators should be dancing around the Maypole together, not having separate celebrations with the Stars and Stripes flying over one gaggle of dancers and the Red Ontario Maple Leaf over the other bunch.

On the other hand, the very mention of such an arrangement tends to be received with loud disquietude on both sides of the border, and the older I get the more I seem to need to have peace and quietude in the head as well as in the breastbone region. And the older I get the more finely attuned I become to the processes of mind whereby such ease of mind, such contentment, is delivered: it is when the mind replays the words, the pictures, the sounds, the smells, the touch-feelings, the tastes of the way it was *with me*, in my own homeland, the prairied part of Saskatchewan.

It seems to happen naturally, this casting back to one's experiences in earlier times. It is as though the mind courted by the spirit is preparing some sort of computer program to take us serenely home. Home to the finer dimensions, the worlds of order and learning many of us have spent most of our fourscore and ten years disputing, disallowing, denigrating and denying.

In the case of Spring, the natural process of mind presents to me the Springs that Larger Mind has stored but it presents them only under certain conditions. Being out "on the land" when the events of Spring are happening is, of course, the surest. When you are walking in the bush and come upon the first crocus of the season in a small clearing there your body and then your mind presents you with the same little startle of pleasure delivered in the same way when you were seven years old and sent off to the safe cow pasture to find a furry purple surprise for your mother who likely could no longer put up with your energetic shenanigans of the day and so had invented a passion for crocuses on the spot to get you out of her hair for an hour or two.

Water running is another. I don't mean running water. Running water comes from a tap and is a part of the "manufactured" part of our memories. Water running is natural. When things are ready in the natural world, why, water runs. And if your early experiences of Spring run-off were stored during your impressionable years on a little Saskatchewan farm, Spring will not have "sprung" for you if you are walking the dark pavement of Moose Jaw, Saskatchewan, though a Chinook has sprinted in with a welcome surprise and running water, darker than the streets, is roaring down to the river via efficient sewer lines that are not permitted to freeze up and disallow their duty.

To relive the Springs that have patterned your soul you have to get down to the river. To the coulees. Ravines, we used to call them, where I came from. The one that cut through our place just east of Saskatoon was pretty shallow compared to the spectacular coulees of south Saskatchewan cow country and, in fact, has been cultivated and disciplined into simply "the low spot" in those old fields by now.

During my early childhood years there was not a lot of water running down that ravine. I know that as a "fact," in the left-hand part of my head. But in the feeling side of that same head there is stored the sound of water running with swishes and gurgles and rushes and twinkles just north of the house beyond the garden. The memory boxes in the creative right-hand mind spring open to present the dialogue of grown-ups announcing "the north way" out of the yard (the way to Gramma's) was out of bounds for a while and that, no doubt, the near well would be flooded clean over its cribbing and the far well would have to be trekked to for house water until the Spring run-off was over and done.

I would not be able to resist the call of water running. It is always just about dusk, the way the mind re-presents the event. The air has the smell of wet new grass and wet old leaves and, almost, the magical foreign smell of ozone just as on sunny winter days when you are outside prying frozen longjohns and snow-white petticoats and sheets off the washline for your mother. I do not ask anyone to come with me. I was an insular child, happy within my own worlds, and had no need, it seems, to be in the company of other living beings. If the current farm dog chose to come along, well and good, but it was better alone.

Water running was a feeling. It was *being* water running. It was yourself drifting into the electrical happiness that buzzed with a Northern Lights sound about your ears in a circling, circling, circling until you felt you had to ground your body by walking robot-like into the edges of the water lest you take off out of that body and soar into the heavens far from the earth and far from the water running its magic down and into the welcoming bodies of the fields and sloughs and little creeks.

A good many years after that first happened to me I had the experience again. I was working in what southern Saskatchewanians call "North Saskatchewan" but isn't. It is bush country, though. And it was the time of the Spring run-off.

I had worked hard all day doing a school visit to talk to young people about their creative minds and to tell some stories and read them others, and to encourage the students to do so too. Then I had driven the little Tercel — through the pine tree green and old-winter-snow white and some resurfaced, subtle, last-autumn colours of that fine country — to the farm where I was to be billetted for a couple of days while working with adult writers in the next town down the line.

It was too early to present myself. I could see the family having seven fits at having to entertain a stranger three hours ahead of the appointed time, so I parked the car on a solid gravel approach and went walking.

I heard water running. I followed the sound. It was the same haunting and magical melody I remembered as a child. Up the road it had overrun the banks of a narrow ravine and was flooding a field where horses paused in their nip-picking of stray new blades of grass to saunter over to the fence to question my presence with calm and interested gaze. The water was defining itself a new way across the grid as inexorably as time defines the lines on the faces of determined prairie folk. The air was crystal clear and carried a faint lovely fragrance of horse.

I don't know how long I stood there being a part of it but when I got to the farmhouse someone said, "We were about to send the Mounties out for you!" A nice Saskatchewan kind of thing people here have been saying to each other ever since I was a kid to pretend they were not really worried about you — and to let you know they care.

Yes, yes, the way Spring springs to mind seems to have a lot to do with how we experienced our first ones. And where.

Does it seem to you I am quite content most of mine happened in Saskatchewan, that *sometimes* green and pleasant land?

# The Trouble with Angels Is

The trouble with angels is they don't have sense enough to stay out of your head. And/or out of your life. I know some people who can see their angels and I know some who can feel them. "Yep, there she is, back again, roosting on my shoulder like a Leghorn hen settling in for the night!" But I can't do either. I am doomed to suffer hearing them. Hearing them mostly inside the head. Which results often in a quandary. "Is that simply my own head chatter giving me quaint surprises or have I (Oh God, again!) been entertaining angels unawares?"

And being rude (again!) to him/her/it. Sometimes you can tell the gender of your angel and sometimes you can't: it all depends. More on this later, I half-way promise you.

It's like this. When you have been trained by life and by an efficient mother to be always extremely courteous and kindly to your earthly brethern (the sistern, too), over the years sometimes your patience wears a little thin. But to be discourteous or unkind to any other human being would be a motherly no-no. And so you take it out on the one who lives inside you.

For a lot of years, then, you take that Inner One to task about being stupid, and about being late, and about being unattractive, and about having paid too much for something you didn't really need but only wanted. And your inner dialogue, your head chatter, when you finally learn to listen to it, is really kind of a killer whale, growing and growing in that verdant ocean of negatives and lolling about ready to whap you with the final permanent whap when you are finally as defenceless as a featherless baby bluebird fallen into a conference of cats.

But that's OK, in a way. Because then you are prime meat for these most peculiar beings called angels. Because that's when they start sidling onto your mind patterns and riding into your inner ear to whisper, "Hiya, Sweetie! I just love it when you saw wood!"

It's true. There you are, minding your own business, which is the business of telling yourself that you have no business to be this, or to do that, or to have said something else to somebody who is now likely pretty busy telling everybody else within the confines of Mother

Earth and Kingdom Come what you have recently injudiciously allowed. And suddenly, overtop the worded natter-natter-natter going on inside your grey matter and overtop the angry grating of the old hand wood saw you hear, inside your own head, "Hiya, Sweetie, I just love it when you saw wood!"

I wouldn't know what to make of it if I hadn't gone "sort of" crazy a few years back and undergone an individualized pressure cooker kind of training to listen for the voices that are foreign to my own head. The alien strains are surprising, interesting, and — I'm content to say — a heck of a lot smarter than I am.

The trouble with angels is they know it. Another trouble is they talk to each other inside your own personal head and are not above teasing you a little if you are being stubborn and wayward again. "Now, now, let's give her a little hand here, our little girl promised to take this old poplar cheese cutter into town to get it sharpened but I see it's still as dull as a butter knife, so let's apply a little muscle, guys!" And all at once my puny biceps will bulge — well, OK, not *bulge,* but at least announce their presence — and that saw will move to beat sixty until I have to smile for the very unusualness of the demonstration.

That's how they put it. They tell me they have *demonstrated* their presence and if I were not so Saskatchewan-stubborn I wouldn't have to be demonstrated to over and over again as if I am a laboratory scientist who won't get any more funding unless forty thousand proofs have been carried out for what half the world knows already anyway: Angels *are*.

The way to lose touch with your own personal angel(s) is to quit living alone in the country and go take a job in a city where the demands for your presence amongst the general population are so high that you begin chasing yourself two weeks *before* you get installed into the workplace. The trouble with angels is they don't care if you lose touch or not; they're a real cavalier bunch who have just as good a time in your head whether you're with them or not.

The trouble with that is, their opinions and unsolicited advice sometimes don't stay safely in your head, they are blurted from your mouth in a way that utterly surprises.

Now you take for example the time this one particular job I'd got was only about two weeks old and the library had made arrangements for me to visit city council. Well, of course, the *library* hadn't. That library was so old and decrepit and out of it that it couldn't have made arrangements to breathe any longer, let alone make arrangements for anything or anyone else to do anything at all. The chief librarian had made the arrangements or had had someone who was paid to do such things make them.

All I was supposed to say when I met this city council was, "Thank you very much for supporting your local committee's application to place Saskatchewan's Resident Writer program in your city for the coming year." Period.

City council was supposed to be talking about getting on with its ten-year-old plans to build a new library. Imagine the surprise of those waiting in the wings to give thanks for this, or to petition for further blessings, when, instead, a new and fantabulous tourist spa began to materialize out of councillors' mouths. For two hours. The word *library* had not once been mentioned.

Inside my head twenty giggling angels were holding their own council meeting. The only way to present a façade of sanity in such situations is to press some kind of Red Alert button and shut them off. It's easier, I must say, than shutting out a city council determined to be collecting tourist dollars by next spring if not by last Wednesday.

The trouble with all that was that suddenly a librarian was poking me in the ribs and telling me the podium was mine. It was so late at night by then and I was so groggy that my first instinct was to grab it up and walk off with it into the night. It was, after all, made of gorgeous light-coloured oak and looked as if it could fetch a couple of twenties at a pawn shop.

I grabbed the podium and hefted, but it was set as solid as a light-fingered gambler's feet in a bucket of mafia cement, so I opened up my mouth instead.

And this giddy angel was thereupon heard telling city council that for the last two weeks of 32 degrees plus I'd been stripping down to unmentionables just to survive in my second-floor office in the old library councillors seemed determined not to mention and that council would get by a heck of a lot cheaper if they'd just go ahead and build a new library and then charge the tourists to come and sweat in the old one. Then, dismayed at what I'd heard from my own mouth, I beat a hasty retreat.

The next day the librarians claimed I had been applauded. Instead of saying, "But it wasn't *me*, it was this stupid angel inside my head!" I said, "Does that mean I still have a job here?"

They said *Yes* and I went back to chasing myself and Saskatchewan Writing round and round the chokecherry bush again. But I told that angel off, I can tell you.

The trouble with angels is, they don't care. They are just so laid back and full of beans and pepper! (Though one of mine claimed one day she could operate much more efficiently inside my head if I cut the salt *and* the pepper out of the daily diet entirely; naturally I told her to go pepper her angelic head, if she had one.) These pesky angels live life so cool they don't care if you think they have made a fool of you again — they just say it was fun and they're not the least bit sorry.

About a week after that council business I came back for a few days to my little house here in sandy poplar-bush country. I had to do some things to get the place ready for the winter. All of Saskatchewan was gold and blue under a sunny sky and after a prime and full harvest. All the way home my head was determinedly full of "job stuff": the next newspaper column, the next school visit, the next writers' workshop, the next office caller's precious book manuscript.

But it was cool in the house when I got here and it is kind of a rule not to burn the wood stacked in the kitchen or even in the back porch if it is not raining and there is a deadfall pole drawn up on the saw horse as sacrifical victim to my body's comfort.

So, overall-clad, with hightop boots drawn on to save the ankles from persistent late spear grass, I was soon out and sawing. I did not notice the words of the workaday world spilling out of my head like so much sawdust; I did not notice the velvet nothingness that took their place.

But suddenly, there She was. "Hiya, Sweetie! I just love it when you cut wood!"

What the heck. I stopped. Hung the saw onto the end of the pole. Blew the schnozz heartily since I am somewhat allergic to sawdust. Grinned. I can get a replay on the good feeling of that grin without half trying.

"Was it you played the fool at city council?" I said.

"Now, Gertrude, would I do that?"

"I'm asking."

"I'm not telling."

"Who cares?"

"Not I!"

A long pause. You get sort of floating when an angel comes to visit and your lungs are full of good oxygen and ozone and your sinuses have just been resoundingly cleared.

"I can smell the old leaves, Gertrude. The essence is quite lovely."

"They're dead. They're dying."

"They are being recycled. Just like you, Sweetie. We can hardly wait, the party's already planned and your mother says she has a lot to tell you."

The light bulb lit up. Incandescent as all get-out.

The last few years of her life my modest and unassuming mother suddenly began to take nothin' from nobody. It has been said, at times, into my head by an angel or two that my mother tries to visit me but that she finds it difficult to read my wavelength.

"Has my mother been to any spas lately?" I asked. I was grinning wider than Alice's Cheshire Cat; there was nothing left of me but grin.

The angel laughed. I know this one well, particularly her laugh; it sounds like the tiny bells that get you in the mood for the long *Hu-ohm* in a Tibetan monastery. Then she left.

I'm dying to know who or what she really is. And I often hear from this angel John who is quite sincere and dependable and who seems to know an awful lot. But the trouble with angels is they will never snitch on each other. So it's best not to even ask.

# Free-Traded Thanksgiving

When I was going to a British Imperial Empire school in farming Saskatchewan, we non-British kids learned to love the British monarchy with an undying passion. In fact, it infected — there are some who would say it *infested* — our non-British mothers too, and their interest in "The Royals" I subsequently saw matched on this side of the water only during the time of King John F.K. and his Camelot south of the border when Americans confessed they were trying to make a sort of royalty out of their first family because they had a passion for bluebloods.

When I was going to a British Imperial Empire school in the Dirty Thirties on the hot hard Saskatchewan prairies we learned "God Save the King" by heart before we had to bother our heads about "O Canada." It was a British queen, the durable Victoria, who doured down at us from the south wall between the Britishman, Edward the Seventh, and his good queen, Alexandra. It was the British flag we drew in art period as

School Beginners, because it was easier than Canada's flag, the Red Ensign, and we sang English folk songs like "Do Ye Ken John Peel" heartily and gladly in music period on Friday afternoons just before home-time.

There are many Canadians nowadays who are trying to tell us that that was a bad thing; that we were being made into British subjects instead of citizens loyal to the True North, Strong and Free.

When I was older and the Union Jack and Red Ensign were water under the bridge, if a mixed metaphor might be permitted here, I could see that a Maple Leaf flag might condition the young folks in all parts of Canada to feel they are all part of the same homeland and untainted, so to speak, by any imperialistic influence, but I was also old enough not to have been born yesterday, and as far as I was concerned we were a nation-in-the-becoming that couldn't see the forest for the trees — or the coyote in the henhouse, to offer a slightly closer-to-home wise old saw.

Here's what I'm trying to get at. We weren't being conditioned, back in the old days, only by British propaganda and symbolism, we were cheerfully and unthinkingly trading any chance we might have had to make a solid nation based on our own history and customs — hodgepodge and high-profile British as they might have been — for those of another nation altogether.

From the word *go* — which really means from the time that school boards everywhere were put into the untenable position of having to provide bargain basement-priced textbooks for Canadian children in order to keep the cost of education down enough to suit taxpayers and governments and their bureaucracies — we were being programmed for American ways from our first week in a Canadian school.

At least in Saskatchewan. At least when I went to school.

You take Thanksgiving. No black-hatted pilgrims in baggy pants and buckled shoes ever landed on any Saskatchewan shore in any Mayflower or Cornflower or even The Good Ship Wheatflour, yet we kids were encouraged — sometimes, depending on the teacher, *ordered* — to draw pilgrims and Plymouth Rocks right along with our wheat sheaves and pumpkins when we had Art, Friday mornings, around about Thanksgiving.

I was fond of those pilgrims and those Plymouth Rocks, and I kept a copybook with their pictures in it, and drawn by my own seven-year-old hands, in a cupboard in my mother's house for nearly twenty years until she finally consigned it to more permanent storage courtesy of a City of Saskatoon garbage truck when she was planning to move to Kelowna.

But I marvelled again at the pilgrims I had drawn so many years ago in that old copybook not too long before it disappeared forever; and I marvelled, too, at the pilgrims' chickens.

Because one Thanksgiving Day picture I had drawn was absolutely polluted with black-and white-barred chickens pecking at the feet of and hovering in the air all about and around one large, solitary, black-hatted, black-bearded and hard-eyed pilgrim with a silver buckle in his hat band, another in each pantleg just below the knee, and another in each big black flat-toed shoe.

It seems I just didn't know, back then, what kind of a Plymouth Rock the American pilgrims had landed upon. And I'd pretty well bet now that the teacher didn't know either. Or else she was very progressive. Because she gave me an A for it. I shall remember that A forever, for I was so poor with a pencil I could hardly draw a straight line with a ruler back then, any more than I can today.

What marvels me most, though — as the ranching people used to say around Maple Creek and Swift Current — is how the Imperial British School System was satisfied to permit us to become so Yankee-ized in our impressionable years, in the days *before* every school textbook bore a Made in U.S.A. trade mark.

Of course, what was the alternative to such a brave and romantic tradition? Well, just for instance, here's what Thanksgiving Day was *really* like, as far back as I can remember it being a special day at all: It was a day off school, Yippee! And it was a day in the garden — sometimes not-so-Yippee, if it was cloudy and cool and a raw wind was blowing.

It was a day to bring in the last of the corn and the first of the pumpkins and citron and marrow; a day to clear off into fairly neat piles the potato and tomato and pea vines; the time to tie corn stalks into bundles for the cows, and to store them as stooks at the north end of the garden if we were feeling like playing farmer at the end of the day and still had the energy to do it.

I can tell you, by suppertime you were awfully thankful it was going to be school again tomorrow because Arithmetic was suddenly easier to take than culling potatoes; and you were thankful, too, for the supper your mother dished up that last-day-in-the-garden night, hot and full of good smells and always lots of it.

There was never time to roast a turkey or even to stuff a chicken. Supper was more likely vegetable soup or summer beet borscht ("summer" because there was yet fresh dill to go into it) and bread with crusts so crisp you had to dunk them in the soup so they wouldn't cut your mouth if you were still quite young.

But no matter what, your mother always seemed to have made a pumpkin pie or even carrot pie, with only a hint of spice in it because her children were, as she always said, such fussy and finicky eaters.

She never seemed to know who was to blame for that.

She was a dear and funny woman, our mother.

She always put vanilla, never cinnamon — which is, I understand, the spice of choice nowadays for pumpkin pie topping — into the cream she whipped out of the Jersey cow and into her fussy and finicky children atop the pumpkin pie she had somehow found the time to bake for Thanksgiving supper when I was young and being spoiled rotten, along with five other young Saskatchewanians, by a woman who worked far too hard and never seemed to know it.

And for whom I am a lot more thankful now than ever I was in the old days when I was kept busy being thankful for a Plymouth Rock that had no business to try to belong to me and thankful to or for a romantic and hard-eyed American pilgrim.

Yet we live in an era of change. Sometimes, it seems to those of us who are no longer young enough to be champing at the bit of new causes, it appears to be change *for the sake of* change. On the other hand, when walls both figurative and real are being knocked down all around us, perhaps it is time to consider opening *all* borders — including those of the mind — and to replace *all* the old symbols (including union jacks and red maple leaves and fleurs-de-lys and stars and stripes, if not Plymouth Rock and its pilgrims) with one that will serve for all of us indwelling on this planet: the circle.

It stands for the earth, unified and made whole again. It is the holy circle of ever-ongoing life.

And if that doesn't beat a baggy-panted guy with silver buckles on his knees like Bobby

Shaftoe gone to sea, even with the support of a gaggle of black and white feathers, I will eat the lot at one sitting, come next Thanksgiving.

# End of Steel

When I was a kid herding my father's cows along the road allowance to save the hard-put pasture grass, I had not yet heard about The Last Spike and how railroad steel had been laid across the broad and true Dominion in order to unite us all into one country and one people. I guess we believed just about anything, those days.

When I was a kid herding cows, though, I listened hard for the whistle of a certain morning train. Not because I yearned to kick the dust of Saskatchewan from my heels and hop a freight to greener pastures, but because the steamer's whistle meant I could bring the cows in and go to school where you could read your *Anne of Green Gables* without checking every thirty seconds for the whereabouts of wanderlusted cows.

Later we moved to town and our dad got a job as day labourer with the CPR at the fabulous pay of forty-three cents an hour. Plus an annual travel pass to anywhere in Canada. I went with him a time or two. There'd be cronies aboard and they would sing out the names of the towns before we even got to them, and I thought it a fine coincidence that they were named in alphabetical order.

In later years, when I was seeing some of those same towns from a little Toyota, it seemed another happy circumstance that almost each one had a Main Street and a Railway Avenue.

Railway Avenue divided a lot of towns. Geographically speaking. A lot of *other* things have divided towns more seriously, hence the saying "the wrong side of the tracks." Although I must say, no matter on which side you lived in *our* town the *other* side of the tracks was always "the wrong side" — that's how everybody kept self-confidence back then.

During my apprentice years as a wife and mother our small family sometimes travelled "the milk run" home to the city from a little country teacherage in the days when roads were poor — or non-existent — and it was the steel that kept things moving and put people into each others' arms again. Along with the milk cans and egg crates and John Deere tractor parts — and the mail, of course: at least one bag for even the veriest hamlet — we would loll content, obligationless for once, happy to see our world, our kind of people in the small towns we shunted into and out of on our way home.

Well, the small towns are dying; the post offices are being whipped (we might say, *sneaked)* out of even the ones that aren't. Elevators are slammed to the ground, and now, too — all too soon — there will be the end of steel.

Goods go by truck now, monster transports dragging ever larger "pups" tail-wagging behind them, to claw the people's roads into potholeish nightmares.

The end of steel. Which could deliver city folks to become dwellers in peaceful happy small towns and take them speedily to and from work in the city if only we put our minds and dollars to it.

The end of steel. The *last* spike, I pray, in the hard track of change-loss, change-loss, change-loss that is being driven across my heart and mind in what ought to be my years of serenity.

To grieve forever is non-survival, but just now I am, I *am,* in mourning.

# Wow, Saskatoons!

I've never seen so many saskatoons in all my life since I was nine years old and my mother and I went picking at the church picnic grounds about a mile and a half from our place, there on a little Saskatchewan farm in the 1930's.

That's a while ago, yet I still love saskatoons so much I once tried to grow them in a garden that was under my jurisdiction, technically speaking, although actually ruled by weeds and other people's cats and strawberries that had too many feet running all over the place without apology. But I have never seen saskatoons, in all these years, like the ones my mother and I used to pick. Until this past summer.

That was the year that Ellen — who used to be a Story when she lived under the same roof with me — and I picked and canned and froze so many saskatoons we'll have preserves and purple teeth for seven years supposing The Order of All Things never grows another saskatoon berry in all of Saskatchewan.

The saskatoon, I would have you to know, is dealt with in the much-publicized *Canadian Encyclopedia*, the publication some of us ultra jingoistic folk were so grateful to hear about that we signed up for three to make sure they actually got on the market for the benefit of the Canadian young; the encylopedia that went on sale the day after ours arrived for about half the price we'd paid. But then, I suppose it's a little like paying income tax: you bite the bullet and then shoot yourself through the foot with it, having first loaded it into the pistol of Rev Canada, and you do it because you cannot have a country run into the ground by incompetents unless you do your fair share towards supporting the system.

In case others may have elected to simply pay more income tax, rather than invest in the *Canadian Encyclopedia*, permit me to expound a bit. First of all, when you find you are being promised Saskatoon Berry, at the very head of page 1644 of the PAT-Z book, there is a lilt to the Saskatchewanian heart at the realization that the beloved saskatoon is to be honoured finally — publicly and, yes, nationally, at that — in a much-touted all-Canadian massed-info publication.

When your eye slides down the page to enjoy it, you are told to *see* Berries Wild, too bad for you if you've loaned your neighbor down the road the A-FOR section with Berries in it.

By the way, each book of the set has the name HURTIG emblazoned in gold just under the alphabetical caption. Therefore, the Berry book stands on your bookshelf announcing to all who walk by A-FOR HURTIG.

And now and again, when I am up too early in the day to be entirely charitable because I have not called the white angels into play yet, I stand in a stupor looking at this, having got stalled on my way towards the stove to get a fire going. And the thought arises that perhaps it is some sort of "in-joke," in-house rating. In which case it would have to be labelled by me, if not by my angels, as a bit self-congratulatory. Which is likely not so. But if it is, it falls a bit short of humility and class. Or so it seems to me on the clouded mornings when I am not on guard against the "opinion poll" that seems to be operating continually — if the white angels have not been summoned — in one's head.

The saskatoon berry, according to Hurtig *et al.*, is a member of the *rose* family — who'd ever have thought it? — and is said to grow from western Ontario to B.C. and the Yukon Territory.

Well, I am not at all averse to granting the beloved saskatoon safe haven anywhere in the west and the north, but I do take a bit of umbrage to see it go to The Big Bad East along with our feed oats and barley. I know I shouldn't feel that way — or feeling that way, should not say so in print, but what the heck, it is too early in the morning and I am feeling invulnerable just now sitting in a quiet cocoon of a house with a post-saskatoon berry Autumn breeze stealing in at the open window and carrying the essence of green things matured enough now to begin giving up life in order that the principles of The Order of All Things may be promulgated.

I know I ought to be more charitable, because one year the only saskatoons I got were the ones I picked at the Toronto airport during one of those interminably long stop-overs one has to endure if travelling from the East back to "where did you say? Saskatoon? In Manitoba, right?"

Never mind. Beyond telling the reader where the saskatoon grows, Hurtig's book tells us mainly what most of us already know: that the city of the same name was called so from a Cree word for the fruit, and that saskatoon berries were a chief component of pemmican. There is, on the page opposite, a coloured illustration of eight common Canadian wild berries — all of them, to my intense pleasure, found in the West. It is a handsome representation and even fairly accurate.

Pierre Berton shows up too, on the same page and also in colour. He is wearing a very nice shirt.

Fortunately, Mr. Berton's shirt has blue in it. That, albeit of the pale variety, seems to bring us back to the varied and sometimes blue as a blueberry saskatoon, its colour in our minds fed from memory. We do not care which one of the fifteen varieties grew in our dad's south pasture, the one each of us remembers was transplanted to mind directly from the days when we were being nourished securely by our hardy and hardworking mothers as was the saskatoon by its mother, the earth.

My mother fed us much more than saskatoon jam and saskatoon pie and saskatoon preserves. She often added pineapple or banana to the preserving kettle after about the hundredth jar of "the plain kind" had been stored safely down the cool dark cellar. But it is not so much the saskatoon as food for which I remember it so lovingly and so well.

When my mother and I went picking saskatoons, they hung like clusters of purple grapes —

or like purple blueberry eyes, even. "Cats' eyes!" was how Richard and Thelma and Bernice used to congratulate the orbs of the finder when someone had spied an especially delectable cluster while the four of us were picking saskatoons together, just to stuff ourselves, at the small patch at the side of the road that separated our parents' farms. At the bottom of the sandhill road, the road that sauntered easily upwards to meet three other roads at Sandhill Corner.

Sandhill Corner. As beige and drab as a good portion of the prairies.

When I was young I was keen on Anne of Green Gables' surroundings and those of King Arthur — particularly the names of local markpoints, but I saw nothing at all romantic or memorable in the common and plain names that marked my local map.

Sandhill Corner sat about a short half-mile from our place, one way, and if you kept going down that road you came to the local school. Sandhill Corner lay about a mile from our Gramma's another way; maybe a couple of miles from our Oma's a third way; maybe a mile from Jesu's white paint and red velvet church the fourth way.

So, come to think of it now, that Sandhill Corner was likely the hub of a very small and very satisfying wheel when I was a kid and going to pick saskatoon berries with my mother.

I was a difficult child and am now ready to confess it. My sisters told me so for years and I couldn't really believe it, for I seemed to be always doing, fairly amenably, something I didn't want to do, for others. "You were always running away," one of them told me not so long ago. Perhaps she had waited so many years to tell me lest I not be strong enough to handle the news, for in our family it is known that most things that happened to me in my childhood simply never got stored in the brain. "I can't imagine where there was to run off to," this storer of memories said next, "but I was always being sent out to look for you when I had homework or housework to do, and sometimes it was already dark."

I was sorry of course. Sorry she had had to do that and sorry I didn't remember any of it. But by then I didn't mind being told — always rather gently, without recrimination: what Lutheran charity those sisters possess! — because it was all kind of interesting, like reclaiming one's life after some sort of amnesia. In fact, if they ever tell me I once fell down a well and was brought up again only after a close Yay vote from the rest of the family, it will go a long way to explaining why I remember less of our life on that little farm than do even my younger brothers.

So I never really minded when these good women, in our grown-up years, told me, privately, the ways in which I had been a difficult child. But when they took to telling my own children that I used to steal real eggs from the hens to make mudpies, eggs our mother might better have sold, mind you, at twelve cents the dozen to buy us school shoes come September; when they took to telling my own children that I had once jumped off the roof of the barn and sprained my ankle and then told our mother one of the sisters had pushed me when actually they had both been safely and sanely out of my way shelling peas to be done up in beer bottles — for better keeping; when they took to telling other such tales to my moral children about the woman who had promised her progeny purgatory whenever they made the slightest move towards doing the same kinds of things when they were kids, why, I decided it was time to face up to my unremembered sins, and even analyze them.

As it turned out, I could do it, too. I mean, I had been living and learning for quite a few years before I got interested in investigating my own inner workings so it wasn't too hard to understand what was actually being said under the forty-dollar words in psychology books.

I was the third child, you see. And the third daughter. *And* a reader. I couldn't be trusted to do anything in the house, because I'd nearly burned it down once when set to start the morning fire, and I'd put salt instead of sugar in the milk pudding I'd badgered my mother to let me make, once. I broke wedding china when set to dust, and Quaker Oats premium china when bade to wash or dry the everyday dishes.

So finally I was simply sent outside to be useless there, as boys are, where the most harm I could do would be to steal a few eggs to make mudpies.

I have analyzed it thus: I think I have felt a little bit rejected all my life by those of my own gender. And now when I think on it, I see it was more along the line of hardly ever getting to talk to my own mother.

My sisters did. In the house with her they told things and got told things. But I hardly ever got to talk to my own mother.

Except when I went picking saskatoons with her.

She always said she took me along because I was strong and willing and had such good eyes for finding the best and the biggest berries. My sisters told me, though — whenever I'd kicked them black and blue in my sleep again because I was the middle one in the bed but still walking the sandhills in my dreams with my mother — that she took me to keep me out of their hair. Having been baptized "the fighting spear maiden," I rather suspect I kicked twice as hard the next night, my eyes shut tight, and listening. When our mother wasn't around I was, I admit it, unconscionable and uncontrollable.

In the berry patch with my mother it was . . . well . . . nice! The sun would be golden and warm, not hot and red and ugly, because we had come out early, real early, when there was still dew on the spider webs lacing the rosebushes and buck brush and brome grass surrounding the berry patch.

And I was so glad to be with my mother I hardened my heart against the struggling flies caught in those delicate and deadly traps. And if I stumbled with half a Burns's lard pail full of berries and spilled them, my mother never seemed to scold me as my sisters did when I spilled the bowl of peas they'd just shelled for dinner.

I bet I could analyze things here a little more, if I were to dig up one of those psychology books that taught me so much when I was finally old enough to know you never tried to read even an Ellery Queen mystery without a dictionary at the elbow. But I don't think I will bother my head with any more analysis.

I think I will amble this rainy Autumn day up the short hill to the old schoolhouse which serves as a storage building for old car parts and unwanted psychology books and a not-so-old and much-wanted electric freezer. And I shall bring back to this little house a not-so-small glass bowl filled with the blueberry eyes of saskatoon berries.

And once they have been sparkled with white sugar and laced with farm cream — although someone I know who wears a white medical coat would not want me to have it — I shall eat them with relish, having invited my blueberry-eyed mother to journey here from the worlds of soul to enjoy them with her third and wayward daughter.

# Country Road, Take Me Home, or Else!

As long as I never had to get out on Saskatchewan winter roads, except as a passenger, I always rather liked winter. I mean, it meant you no longer had turnips to hoe in the hot sun. It meant there were no mosquitoes requiring slapping. It meant there were no fish coming home every Sunday night in summer or, in the fall, rigor-mortised ducks that needed laying out and some form of embalming.

Winter meant there was time again to read, thank heaven! There was time again to sew and knit and make stuffed animals for the children, but you'll forgive me if I don't get ecstatic about all those things. Not that I didn't do them, I did. But they were my winter penance for sins of other lives and I pretended patience — and even, sometimes, satisfaction — in doing them; pretended so successfully, for the most part, that those around me were fooled by it and asked me to please do more of the same. So much for patience, like virtue, being its own reward: sometimes it's its own comeuppance.

So, all in all, I rather liked winter, and I certainly never worried about how I was going to get wherever I needed to go.

I hardly ever went anyplace, anyway. I lived, in the time I am now talking about, in little country school teacherages with a country school teacher who was rather large and so took up more than his share of room in those cramped quarters. And back then, living the places we did, there really wasn't anyplace much to go except to the neighbours', or to the creek to drown Joe Story's brand new fishing rod whenever he tried to teach me how to cast for jacks in the shallows.

So I pretty well stayed close to home, especially in winter, and when I did not it was the driver's job to get us wherever we were going. I was free to sit back and mentally admire the three days' worth of chores I had done in one morning so that we could get on the road early enough to suit the driver. I could sit back and admire the Christmas card look of farming Saskatchewan, who often dressed herself in a virginal white overcoat, winters, back in those innocent days.

We had a '46 Chev back then. Or at least Joe Story did: back in those days it did not do for a relatively new wife to lay joint claim to a relatively new car. It had a sun visor and it had a fox tail on the aerial. The radio was incidental; it was always needing fixing. The car had frost shields made of glass with electric wires running through them and which, once laminated with the old days' version of Crazy Glue to the front and rear windshield, had to be connected to the battery — if I remember correctly — with yards and yards of wire. And before we could go anyplace in winter Himself would have to be up at four o'clock in the morning to shake down the coal embers of the kitchen stove into its ash pan and carry it out to the car, huddling as best it could as close to the house as possible, for there was rarely a garage came with the living accommodations "package" for country school teachers in those days.

He would crawl under the car with the hot box of hot ashes and place it under and in line with the engine to warm the oil while he came back to bed to warm icy feet and speculate that maybe we'd be best to stay home. I never said *No,* but we generally went anyway; it was always a challenge to him, somehow, to do it.

The February night he had to get me sixty miles to the city because his son was preparing to make a premature entrance into the world, I think he just went out and *dared* the car not to start if it valued its very life. That was about the only time I really *had* to be someplace, and the sooner the better. I lay in the back seat, willing the child to stay where it was until we got there, and never for one second doubted that our chaffeur would get us to our destination.

But now I am the one who has to get me wherever I need to go, and now I seem to need to go a lot of places. Especially in winter.

For the same reasons that I used to have more time for other things besides work when winter fell upon rural Saskatchewan, so now do the people who might want to drive out to their local library to hear a writer and a talker read and tell stories. And so it is in winter, mostly, that one is invited to do just that.

When Joe Story left this planet to become more safely employed in other realms, I could not drive a car. When he had offered to teach me I'd told him, No thanks, I was baking bread and could not leave it to its own devices in order to turn lazy circles in the schoolyard's gopher and badger holes. Once he became very insistent about it.

Who knows? Perhaps there was a part of him that knew he would not be much longer around to do the driving. But I put hands on hips, looked him in the pale blue-grey eyes that had turned many a truant scholar to ice, and said, "Now looka here! I am never going to be going anyplace *you* aren't, and you already know how to drive, so cool it, Buster!"

How was I to know he was going to go, all too soon, some place I wasn't going? Thereby leaving me stranded with two cars, a farm truck, and a motorbike — for none of which I even knew how to turn an engine key.

It hasn't been an easy transition, and now that I need to go more places in one winter than I once did in any ten years when I was being an undemanding passenger, I look upon every stray snowflake that falls as the pure connivance of the pure devil, designed to carry me into hell. Or at least into another car on a slippery city steet or into a deep ditch on a lonely stretch of south Saskatchewan road where you're more liable to see a coyote than another car if it's a stormy forty centigrades below zero.

Only old coyotes, and writers too old to learn to do anything else but write for a living, travel then, it sometimes seems to me.

I have no sense of direction whatsoever. There is not a single grey-cell in my upstairs computer that is marked north, south, east, or west — or even up or down or sideways, for that matter. If I drive out of the King George Parkade in downtown Saskatoon, after I've executed one partial swirl down the ramp the Hudson's Bay store across the road from it has dramatically shifted to the wrong side of the street and I am coming where I should be going, if that makes any sense.

When we had moved into a very small town, after years of living in open prairie country, I even got lost going for the mail, though the post office lay on the same street as our house and the whole street was only about four blocks long. It has even been said, by family members who have had to endure this failing of mine for too many years now, that I can get lost in my own house, simply going from room to room, and there's been a not-so-subtle suggestion that I carry with me a ball of silken thread, like Theseus on his way to interview the man-eating Minotaur.

For a long time I tried to hide this ineptitude from others, particularly those who are willing to pay me to come and speak in their own small towns. I always managed to get there on time, somehow — sometimes with the snow shovel still at the ready on the passenger seat — and I would make jokes about having been stuck in a coulee while going in the opposite direction to my destination. And people always laughed. Which goes to show that the painful truth, brazenly presented, is often the best cover-up there is for stupidity.

Eventually, of course, the truth leaked out. And now the people who hire me often diplomatically send along a detailed hand-drawn map of the town, complete (almost) to every fire hydrant — and maybe even every dog — to help get me where I am supposed to be by a certain time on a certain day.

No one who knows me ever offers me that most frustrating of Saskatchewan expressions, "You can't miss it!" I travel with forty-two road maps off which I write directions on the backs of old envelopes, writ large so the words can be read by the glare of the dash lights: hwy 39 to Pdnk & then rt (Sth!!!) on 6 to rgna (aftr!!! sptnk & not befre). Et cetera.

I'd really be lost without them.

But even so, when the whole world is white — a uniform even unmarked undelineated sea of white white white — and when highway signs and fire hydrants and dogs are all hidden in the same stuff, it's a worry to me the whole time I'm on the road whether or not I'm actually going to make it to Frontier, Saskatchewan (where I'm expected) or wind up in Billings, Montana (where I most certainly am not.)

Mostly I drive Toyotas. And maybe it is only my imagination — or the luck of the draw, or something — but it seems to me the little Tercels who have had me in their care have been more obliging than the other two brands I've experimented with. One of the experiments was along the order of a little wind-up toy car, short-bodied but sitting high off the road in comparison. It almost seemed as though you were going to get to a corner before the hood of the car did, and it was pretty unnerving.

Once I was doing a week's work for Southeast Library Region. This was back in "the good old days" when libraries still had enough money to put a librarian on the road with the visiting author. I had met the headquarters rep at a school in Wood Mountain, as I remember. We did our thing there with a wonderful group of young people and then prepared to go down the line to the next town.

Well, a storm had blown up while we were working with the children, and it was as near to a white-out as I ever want to see. The librarian was driving a big Cougar, courtesy of her father, and

I was driving, as I have said, a little wind-up deal. Courtesy of the Mother Russia, if you must know. And all I can say is, if it had not been for the brake lights of that Cougar flashing into my eyes on a very regular basis I'd have been making a highway of the ditch a hundred times before we reached the next stop.

Then there was that April Fool's Day. I forget the year. The snow was all gone. I drove down to Portreeve, Saskatchewan. That's Cow Country, Man! I went to speechify about Saskatchewan and why I seem to write so many stories about it.

The speechifying was to happen at the eighth annual spring ratepayer's meeting of the Rural Municipality of Clinworth. *Spring* meeting, I said.

The trip down was great, except for those vague intrusions-of-mind with which one is presented, such times. For example: maybe the invitation was an elaborate April Fool's joke (you know how these cow country guys are!), and I might wind up on the steps of the Portreeve Community Hall with no ratepayers, no meeting — and, worse yet, no south cow country roast beef dinner. This was in the days before I knew enough to never leave home without a peanut butter sandwich and a thermos of coffee stashed near the gear shift within grabber's reach.

I needn't have worried. The ratepayers were there, and very friendly. The beef at the bountiful supper was just as good as any my dad ever put on the table. And the meeting was an eye-opener — I'd supposed all cattle folks needed to know about was how to run cattle. So the long and the short of it is that, though my part in proceedings was done shortly after the last swallow of beef and the after-supper coffee, I stayed on to get scared spitless, along with a lot of other people, about Swelling Clay Soils and their Effects on Farm Buildings, which created visions of houses and barns already walking on stilts at one end and digging down to China at the other.

Inside of me a Somebody was saying: Get the hell out of here, there's trouble on the road! But I got stubborn and in return I said — without moving my lips, of course, for I wouldn't have wanted the people of Portreeve to reckon they'd invited a looney to visit their meeting — "Well all right, all the more reason to stay off it then!"

Finally I did hit the road. And on the way home, about the time I hit Kindersley, I got my April Fool joke. Snow and wind and ice and rain and slush. For the next hundred miles I *guessed* at the whereabouts of the road. At Fox Valley I'd have liked to pull into a farmyard that presented itself and sit it out, but I had to be someplace else the next day to deliver another message about the hardiness of Saskatchewanians. And just as I was going to turn into the farmyard a transport loomed up to hiss at the Toyota's rear end.

I prayed it past and then hung onto its tail-lights for dear life. When I crawled, weak as a wet hot noodle and a few sweaty hours later, into bed at home I swore I wasn't going anyplace again on a Saskatchewan road in winter unless I was safely inside a coffin. But I set the alarm anyway.

One autumn, some years later, I went tooling merrily up to the Yukon, serene in the belief that the roads up there might be snowy and blowy but it would surely be too cold up there in The True North Strong and Frigid for winter to wing in on a freezing sleet storm three times a week for the first two months of White World of Wonder. Ha!

Well, I made it through that too, with idiosyncratic vehicles from a government car pool that made every trip out a new adventure. Like the long wide Chevy with all the dials and buttons and whatchamacallits just out of arm's reach and with windshield wipers frozen shut from Whitehorse to Jake's Corner, and with one ore truck every seventeen minutes barrelling down on you either from in front or behind, spewing road gunk as only they know how to spew.

To this day, travelling in winter for me is still nothing but a sea of questions, all of them forbidding: Will the roads have at least a minimum of traction or will they all be ice-skating rinks again? Will the front-wheel drive universals make it or should I have coughed up for regulation winter tires? Will the transport truck breathing down my neck pass me before I come across a jack rabbit blinded by the car lights? Is the shoulder safe to drive on in order to get Mr. Sem-eye and his Dukes-a-Hazzard horsepower by, or is it a sheet of glass underneath that snow cover?

For that matter, is there even a paved shoulder out there? Once, on the road to Regina, I cold-shouldered it to let one of the Big Guys by, only to run out of pavement — where the contractor had run out of dollars, I suppose. It had rained and rained before it had snown. (Please let me say *snown*, I've always wanted to: it seems so right, somehow.) I am glad to say I regained the road. I am glad to say the contractor had to harrow over my ploughed furrows once spring came. I am sorry to say that gravel-plus-Regina-clay shoulder is still extant at the time of writing.

Here's an odd one. Until I sat down to consider what there might be to say about Saskatchewan — or Yukon, or Siberian — winter roads and one's chances of getting back home on them, I really thought I was pretty cool about it all. Chilled out, they're saying nowadays; it makes me smile, I can't help it.

Actually, I'd been driving so long by then that, although familiarity wasn't exactly breeding contempt, it was fertilizing resolve, so that sometimes I could even take to the road without sweating bullets at the first ice patch. And so, though I take umbrage very little, now that I am in those "golden years" people are so fond of lying about, I have to confess to suffering just a little dab of it every time somebody — with the best of intentions, I'm sure — says, "Well, at least if you had a man along with you, but running all over the place in winter at *your* age?"

I always say, as cool as a cucumber left out in the front porch in December, "It's the car does the running, so what's so marvellous about that?"

But now that I've put it all down on paper, I'm beginning to see their point. I have no business to do it anymore, unless I can do it as a passenger.

I wonder if maybe I should advertise in the Personals of the farming papers for a driver, courageous and calm and dependable, with nerves of steel and small enough to fit into a little Japanese eaglet without cussing — or taking his fur hat off.

Maybe I'll just think about that.

# Talkin' Prairie

If you are in love with words but would rather keep them inside your head than tell them, you shouldn't be a writer. If you are in love with "The Prairie West" much more than you should be, given the fact that even Ottawa is trying to become a global village nowadays by communicating a bit more honestly with "the sum of its parts," and if you've determined you *have* to be a writer, you shouldn't write so much about the prairies, it might make others think it's OK to centre their own feelings around their own home region instead of around the wider red-and-white-mapleleafed state.

If you're in love with words and in love with the prairies and are often moved, in spite of good sense, to write down words about words — the words prairie people have been using since the English language came to the western Canadian prairies — why, you should spend a few days first reading something like *A Dictionary of Canadianisms* and thereupon dig out a few prairie words the experts have told us about there. That is the sensible approach.

But if you are too stubborn for words, and lazy, and gone past sixty, what you do instead is research your own head, and you put down on paper the words stored in the memory bank of your own cranium and in the glowing recesses of your own prairie heart.

There's the *sod house* or *soddie,* for example. The same complaint is made over and over about sod roofs as is made about the soldier-built trenches of wartime: after it has rained three days in a row outside them, it rains another week *inside* them.

Somebody who must have been doing a little research on that very subject asked me once how many sod houses I had lived in as a kid. Since I was somewhere in my forties at the time of asking I had a little trouble taking the question as gracefully as I might have. In fact, I was quite rude about it. I was not yet at the time, let us say, living in grace. So I said, "Look here, Buster, I'm not an old pioneer, I just *look* like one." But I knew the question was a comeuppance for having ignored my mother's advice about wearing a sunhat against the sun whilst picking field rocks and about never going to bed before you had graced your skin with some sort of grease.

My mother had gorgeous skin; everybody who knew her commented on it. She had it, she used to tell me — when presenting me with another pastel-coloured jar of experimental skin cream — because every day of her life she had taken her own advice, and, "if I couldn't afford even plain old Woolworth's cold cream I would use cow cream; so here, use this, it's supposed to be good and it claims to have cow cream in it; your lines are already starting to show."

Anyway, I never saw virgin prairie though I once met a young woman named Virginia Prairie, as true as I live: she was from Minnesota. And I never saw a sod house, either, until a long time after I had left the farm with my parents; there just weren't too many sod houses left when I was born, supposing there had been any thereabouts to start with.

Any there might have been, and left standing unattended, would certainly have had leaky roofs by then.

I'm not sure why I'm so obsessed by the leaky roofs of sod houses. It likely has to do with the fact that most of my adult life I have been a compulsively neat housekeeper. It has to do with being lazy: if you clean every day you don't have to marathon clean in spring and fall like everybody else, and so wear your nerves — and your bones — to a frazzle.

Since I cannot abide a sticky bit of jam on the kitchen linoleum even though I'm still spry enough to step over it, I have got stuck in the idea that nothing so exemplifies the hard lot of pioneer women as a doggone leaky roof coupled with a dirt floor. Or even a leaky roof and a board floor.

I suppose one could be facetious and say, well, it rained so little in those days there wasn't much danger of stomping with your feet in the Saskatchewan prairie mud in order to get from your bed to the stove to get the flapjacks going for breakfast. But of course that wasn't so. In the early years of settlement there was good moisture most years; it isn't fair to keep our mind-set in the grey days of the Dirty Thirties.

All the more reason for roofs to leak back then, and sometimes it made a woman's lot hardly bearable. What could be worse than living inside an earth house like a mole? Living inside a *wet* earth house like a gopher, that's what, a gopher flooded with slough water from both its doors by sharp-eyed schoolboys — yes, yes! and girls, of course — bearing five-gallon lard pails and stout maple sticks.

One such gopherized woman, fairly newly arrived from a jolly old European country where the people are addicted to horses, had tried to ride to the hounds here at her new "home" on a green-broke bronco. Her ankle had been so badly shattered that it couldn't be splinted properly by the local sawbones so it had to be confined within a homemade, cotton batten-filled, half-a-coffin kind of cast. Needless to say not only her ankle was confined, she was too. The bed was her half-a-coffin.

There'd been plenty of rain, so whenever it began to do its raining indoors she had to hold an umbrella over her head to escape the most of it and the children were strictly commissioned to play only under the umbrella of the kitchen table. (I don't know why I say "kitchen table," for that supposes a kitchen, doesn't it? and most of the soddies were only one room.)

Sod roofs came down around the ears of people when rains rained too hard and too long on them, when cows walked overtop of them, when the supporting poplar poles rotted through and gave up the ghost and, incidentally, the roof.

Not everybody had to build of sod back then, of course — only those who lived on the open plains too far from any kind of logs or planed lumber. But anybody who wanted to farm the prairies had to *bust sod.* That is, plough up the prairie. For a lot of Easterners — Canadian Easterners, I mean — *sod buster* or *clod buster* is still the favourite term for their western cousins. Next to *stubble jumper* or *prairie chicken.*

People who took up homes in bush country were called — or dubbed themselves — *bushwhackers* or *trailblazers. Trailblazers* sounds very romantic and all that, very James Fenimore Cooperish, in fact. Bushwacker is more prosaic. Likely closer to the facts, too. I mean, if you went whacking away at bush all day — sometimes with a dull axe because you didn't know any better — you soon knew all about blood, sweat and tears. All of them your own; the blood extracted not usually by the axe, but by millions of mosquitoes.

The people in north Saskatchewan bush country jolly well built houses of logs or of lumber. But on the plains you *busted* the tough, root-infested surface sod in long fourteen-inch furrows. No, *you* put it into metric if you need it; the sod busters didn't metric their ploughshares and their measurements so I'm not going to do it either! The sod sometimes came from a dried-out slough bottom. Easier cutting.

Then you split your long row of sod into lengths you could handle without them falling apart at the grass-rooted seams, and from them you built your sod shed, sod house, sod shanty, or soddy. Then you wrote home and told your mother or your sweetheart or your wife that it was safe for her to come on out to the prairies because now you had a home for her. One such wife "turned away after first glance so that he would not see me crying," but there were many so glad to have the family reunited they would have lived in a hole in the ground. In fact, some of them did.

Others lived in that hole *on top* of the ground, the sod shanty. If you were really lucky, your lady partner was there and helping you build it. If you were blessed there were no children for a while to require the umbrella of an heirloom rug, perhaps, over the ninth generation black oak cradle while they napped on a rainy day.

As to why pioneers *bust* the sod instead of more gramatically splitting or cutting or carving or even bursting it, I don't know. *Bursting* is what you actually did to that whole, entire, untouched, ripe and succulent land. You aimed the shining knife of your plough at the promising flesh of the new and hitherto untouched land and laid it open as one does a ripened melon in the field at harvest.

I suppose people *bust* the sod a hundred years ago for the same reasons their free-wheeling descendants bust balloons or nearly bust themselves laughing or bust somebody a good one on the nose. Frontier types simply can't stand to "talk fancy" in case that smacks of giving in to authority, even if it is only the authority of the schoolhouse. And besides, to use schoolbook grammar might lead others of our own kind to suspect we aren't tough enough and rough enough to handle ourselves in this rough and ready land.

*Prairie* is a lovely word, a glowing one, one filled with good and warm and all-positive feelings. Like *home* and *mother* and *fresh*. Nowadays it is a word used deliberately in advertising to attract the heart of potential customers so that you can thereby attract their wallets. Just consider: FRESH BAKED BREAD FROM DOWN-HOME PRAIRIE WHEAT. Doesn't that get you right in the old pump? To say nothing of the old bread basket.

In the not-so-bad Good Old Days *prairie* was often used to help make a hard life a little more endurable by putting a little humour in it.

There's one *prairie* term I wouldn't even mention, let alone talk about, except that not to do so would be to invite scathing comments from a lot of jackknife veterinarians to the effect that "she calls herself a writer, but she don't do no research."

That interesting colloquialism is *prairie oysters*. I know all about that, I just don't want to tell about it. How my ma's Uncle Bill used to come over the hill on a fine green May morning when the colts were ready to be cut, or my dad was ready to *have* them cut, for I don't suppose the colts were ever consulted. And I'm not going to talk about it because then I'll have to confess that one time I hid behind the woodpile out of a terrible curiosity and saw those colts being lassooed and thrown and held and cut and then something white and muscled and shaped like two oblonged eggs joined together was thrown off over the cutter's shoulder to land too near me for comfort. I didn't know what the heck it was all about but as soon as I had crawled out of earshot I threw up.

The other *prairie oyster*, the kind I *am* going to tell about, was not very nice, either, and so if you want to skip the next part I don't blame you.

How shall we do this? Well, let's say it is back in the not-so-bad Good Old Days on the Saskatchewan prairies and you are living there. And one day your mother is feeling *peserich* again. *Peserich* is kind of prairie talk too, if you are from the *German* Saskatchewan prairies. It means "somewhat ailing, but not critically ill." It is a word used by the kind of people who would say "bust" instead of "burst", if you see what I mean. It is not to be found in Dr. Erich Weis's half of the two-volume Schoffler/Weis *Deutsch-English Worterbuch,* produced in smoky, industrious, practical-minded Stuttgart, in West Germany, where, the university towners in Tuebingen to the south might claim, the people say things like *peserich* instead of *unpaslich* and wouldn't think of apologizing for doing so.

If you were a young married woman back in the old days of prairie Saskatchewan and were feeling *peserich* it might be that you were in the family way, likely a wonder-full thing if it was the first time. But if you were living on a small dirt farm and had three or four already, too bad.

But an Auntie Myrtle or Tanta Irmgard would come over to help cook for the threshers, if it was that time of year, and to prescribe a daily prairie oyster to help build you up. The aunties never called it a prairie oyster, it was the young brash uncles, or even the proud — or shame-faced — expectant father who did that.

First thing the helper did was open a can of store tomatoes. Whenever we had canned tomatoes at our house I used to wonder if my Uncle Emil had put the label on it, for he had moved East by then and was working in a tomato canning factory — but that's another story. If an auntie was going to fix you up with your first curative prairie oyster and there were not good red ripe tomatoes to be had from your own garden, she would open a can of the store-bought kind and begin.

She drained about three fingers' worth of red scarlet juice into a tall tumbler, then broke an egg into it. Then she said, "Here, drink it, and try not to break the egg."

Well, I nearly flipped. As did a lot of *peserich* women's innards, from all reports. Including my mother. Such a woman was too fastidious. But if she was also *peserich* she might stir it all up with a fork and add some salt and a hint of fresh dill from the garden and a dash of tabasco. And call it a tonic and drink it each day.

And when the child was born s/he would be fat and blooming, and as rosy pink as a young tomato already ripening on the vine.

I've been feeling *peserich* too, of late, although not too likely to become a biblical Elizabeth in the Nursery Miracle department. But I made a prairie oyster the other day using a supermarket egg priced at a dollar nine the dozen for smalls. I almost always buy the smalls partly because, in my terms, an egg is an egg is an egg so why pay twenty-four cents more to pretend it isn't. But this time I bought the smalls partly because — unlike my mother and other fastidious clients of the prairie oyster cure — if the directions say not to, I am not a stirrer.

I shan't have another. Supposing the alternative is to die a lingering death. And the operative message here is: If you insist on going back to the good old days for a cure for feeling *peserich,* go all the way back. Back to the country where you can get an egg direct from a hen, with no middle-man in on the act, so that your prairie oyster will look at you from the tumbler round and full and firm with its one good yellow eye, not flat and stale and unprofitable as are all the things of this world, including the things that come inside a twelve-section pasteboard carton, once you are past sixty. And even at that, don't forget the dill and the tabasco.

Now that I've reached the age where humans tend to inspect the things of this world with a somewhat baleful eye, the memory bank seems to be spilling out, more and more, of an early morning's arising, the world of "the old days." In the 1930's, when I was walking in my dad's south pasture, I didn't give a ding-dong about the old days, unless they were old enough to have produced gnomes and fairies. For that is what I was looking for in the south pasture. Not purple coneflower or woods violet or sturdy goldenrod. Or even the cows I'd been sent to fetch home for the milking.

Because the regulation, school-history "old days" did not beguile me, I didn't know until forty years later that when I was a kid I'd walked nearly every day over the ancient grave of a dead man from the *really* old days, those times when I went hunting after cows, and that he'd perhaps hunted buffalo in the very draw where those creatures often hid from me. Quite successfully.

*Buffalo* is an intriguing word and if you are the kind who can still commit yourself to checking things out you'll find, in a book that purports to name only things truly Canadian in origin, four and one-half pages of things named after the buffalo.

The buffalo seems to have been named in stages, with speculative pauses in between, and then on to a different turning. Just like Mother Nature made the real thing, starting out with the lean and mean idea in mind and changing course just before creating those massive shoulders. In 1583 there was a report of a "Beaste, much bigger than an Oxe, and . . . supposing it to be a certaine kind of Buffe." The hides of Buffe the reporting party found they took back to France. The French word for buffalo is *buffle*. Where the French got the name when they didn't have the game, so to speak, is beyond my ken and caring.

Anyway, I don't mean to talk about the buffalo bean or the buffalo berry or the buffalo wool, or the buffalo coat or horse or head or knife or tent or lick or jump, all of which I have at least seen in my lifetime, I mean to talk about the buffalo chip. Because it had more meaning in my life, let's say, than all those others put together.

In fact, by the time I was set to collecting them, our pasture hadn't been the home where the buffalo roam for so long there wasn't a hope in hell of finding even a buffalo skull which, I gather, has a bit more permanence than has whatever comes out of the leaner end of the buffle. But there were lots of cows by then and, while you won't find four and one-half pages in even a purely cow book about the things named for and after cows, there were certainly about four and one-half wagon boxes of cow chips, all told, in my dad's cow pastures.

Well sir, one day some city young folks came out to visit. They came with their folks. Teenagers certainly did not have their own set of wheels in those days — they were only too glad if the old man had a Model A with so much as a bald set of tires. And the two girls, Merna and Nan, came along with me to fetch the cows home. And they got into a real fight, a dandy hit, jab, push, and throw one.

There were a few tears, too. One of my own sisters was there too and as I remember it we just stood back and watched the whole thing as if it was a movie. And when we finally got home with the cows Merna burst (she didn't *bust)* into the barn ahead of the cows where her city-dressed dad was forking hay into mangers with my own dad. And as the rest of us slapped the cows through the door we heard her beller, "Daaa-dee! Nan threw buffalo chips at me and look, she caught me right in the hair with it and Mommy only just washed it with Blondex before we came out!"

And my sister and Nan smiled and didn't even offer protest. But I pursed my lips real tight, I was very moral in those days, because Merna was a liar. And soon said so, in unusually hearty manner. What Nan had thrown was a plain old cow pie, no harm to the Blondex ringlets, either, because it had been as old and grey and dried-paper looking as an old wasps' nest. And when cow pies had got to that stage you could pick them up bare hands — for only cowboys and ladies carried gloves with them wherever they went in those days — for making a fire whilst picking berries or on a picnic, and nobody even sent you off to a slough to wash your hands, after.

Cow pies were cow pies. *Chips* were the bits and bites of wood my dad left around the chopping block when he cut the needle nose end on to willow fence pickets. Chips smelled nice and cool and pungent, and when you had chips you needn't cut a stove wood chunk into kindling, always a time waster. An old and leaky calves' feeding pail full of them was enough to cook a quick dinner on a hot day, if you were satisfied with leftovers.

Anyway, when that dried-up old cow pie hit tattletale Merna in the Blondexed hair it broke into bits, into itsy bitsy bits, not chips. And Merna was therefore a sorehead and a liar, and I liked Nan after that even better than ever.

But I know a little more than I used to about a lot of things. I know about the places on the prairie where wood was so scarce and the winters so long that, no matter how many buffalo chips you might have stacked in a rough-built lean-to to help out during the cold snaps, the winters were so long and so severe that at least in one case in the deep southwest a family, unbeknownst to its far-flung neighbors, had to tear down the barn, board by board and timber by timber, to keep from freezing to death in the big drafty house old country money had built for them when they had first come out, to start anew on a "free" homestead in the colonies.

When I first read about people shooting buffalo in the early days just for their tongues I was so angry at the waste of the meat that I could not think straight for three days. I couldn't even imagine how many would have to bite the dust in order to make forty pounds or so of the "delicacy." But I have put my mind to work lately, just for the practice, to show me what it would take to fire up an old Quebec heater to keep the frost from taking over this small and reasonably well-insulated house sitting within a good shelterbelt of low-slung maple.

If you're going to do it with flat old disks of dried-up dung, the pictures-of-mind show, that takes one heck of a lot of buffalo!

And, on what I sincerely hope is a related subject, it takes one heck of a lot of promotion — in the classroom, in the kitchen, in the factory and office — to rid the language of a word that is not a word. Let me sneak up on an example of that.

They say Latin is making a comeback. High time, too, I say. Here on the prairies we could use a dead language. There's a little too much life in our own, people tell us. It has to do with errors. We make mistakes when we talk, here in catch-as-catch-can Saskatchewan where we speak quite cheerfully about letting the devil take the hindmost because we mean to be out in front and out of the way of the pitchfork; we make mistakes and we just don't give a good goldarn, we keep talkin' *irregardless*.

When I showed up in a city school, having been subjected by then to a baker's dozen years of exposure to unadulterated farm type "prairie talk" with all its slang and colourful shortcuts, I wanted to learn to talk like an Englishman — or at least a Canadian university professor, *irregardless*.

Everybody else did too. Or if they didn't want to, it didn't matter, they got English grammar and spelling and pronunciation along with English flags and poetry and history *irregardless.*

I admired the English language and, by association, the English, so much I adopted their diction, their grammar and their mind-set (as I rather suspect now) wholeheartedly to say the least. I was delighted when the mothers of school acquaintances said, "What part of England did your people come from then, dear?" And I was as embarrassed as all get-out when I brought a veddy English chum home from school one day and my mother served bara hai and apple strudel on thick German platters *irregardless.*

I was even more embarrassed when I got to high school and the teacher of English Composition advised me, most gently, that the word to use for "having no regard or consideration for" was regardless. There was no such animule as irregardless in the entire menagerie of the English language, he said. When he said "animule" he smiled in a way that tipped you off to the fact that if you ever said it he'd find a way to tell you, most gently, that there is no such animule as animule in the entire English language.

Well, that all threw me for a loop, regardless. Not only my dad and my storytelling uncles back on the farm, but the CPR switchmen in the town where we lived, and the car cleaners and milkmen and car repairmen and grocers — they all said "irregardless."

But I swallowed my embarrassment as best I could and slunk *(slank* is archaic; don't use it!) into Latin class next, where I found out in short order that *ir* is a prefix screwjiggered onto a good sound Anglo Saxon word. And it comes from the Latin *in,* meaning "not." The Latin teacher had been off sick for three days because the guys in class had badgered him into demonstrating his wrestling holts. He'd been some sort of champion in Varsity wrestling. And by the way, *Varsity* should be an outlawed word too, in my books, regardless.

The guys liked to get the Latin teacher to demonstrate his wrestling holts (I know about *holts* as an ixnay word, but honest to Pete, I love it and I just can't help it) because then he would forget to demonstrate the subjunctive perfect passive — or worse still, ask *them* to do it.

The whole thing was just too bad. If he hadn't been off sick he'd have spilled the beans about the *ir* in *irregardless* soon enough to save me from the gentle persuasion of that dreamboat of an English teacher. There are English teachers who haven't an English gene in their bodies, so why isn't everybody saying "teacher of English," if I may be so cheeky as to ask?

Oh dear. Do I hear you saying, "So what? The language is changing and some of us use it incorrectly but we seem to understand each other. So, so what?"

Well, I'll tell you so what. The other day I decided I needed a new dictionary. It seems I keep putting too many *u*'s into words nowadays to suit certain Americanized Canadian editors I write for. Their *honors* and *colors* and *harbors* still come out of my mental programmer with an o-u-r at the end, and it's getting quite frustrating.

So I went out and bought a *Funk & Wagnalls* Up-to-Date and Reliable, General Purpose, Canadian, Authoritative, College Dictionary (thumb-indexed yet) for seventeen, ninety-five.

And just for the peculiar benighted hell of it I went looking for *irregardless*.

It was there too! Page 715, in case you are one of those purists and don't believe me. The editor said it is an adverb. It means "regardless." It is, he said, "a nonstandard or humorous usage."

Maybe so. But I didn't suffer public embarrassment in front of thirty-three grade nines whose dads were all doctors and dentists and teachers of Mathematics and English, all those years ago, to have it all go down the drain now. And I'm not gonna git caught usin' the dang thing again, regardless!

It's a funny thing — funny-odd, not funny-ha ha, as we used to say as kids — how one's own personal and private computer stores certain words and spills them out for us to use at what it considers the appropriate time; how it refuses to accept others and simply kicks them on and through the system unceremoniously, into oblivion, as if we had never heard of them.

Now, *good-bye* is a common word; plain, simple, useful. Yet when I was a kid hardly ever did I hear anybody say *good-bye,* and the first time I ever saw it in written out in a book I wondered if it was an error by the makers. The wondering almost unnerved me because when I was a kid the makers of books were the presenters of truth almighty. If it stood in a book it was correct. It had to be. If it wasn't — didn't our fathers and uncles tell us so often enough? — somebody would take the printer to court, sure as shootin'. So trust them, said the fathers and the uncles, if you saw it standing in a book, if you saw it even sitting in the newspaper, it was so.

But anyway, there stood this word *good-bye* and it was a wonderment. Mostly our people said *aufwiedersehen* when they left you — or *wiedersehen* if they were in a hurry — and that was an awful mouthful. And then we got to hate things German because there was a war going on and it was the popular thing to show how patriotic you were by downgrading everything that was krautish.

And so we wouldn't say *aufwiedersehen* even to our omas. We maybe said *So long!* if we'd been to enough movies, but mostly we didn't. We didn't say good-bye either, we just went.

Well, a while ago, I went to checking. And it seems to me that most prairie people — or new frontier people, or western Canadian people, or whatever name for us suits you, I'm not fussy — most prairie talkers never say good-bye much, either.

Maybe they're afraid if they do, they'll never ever see you again. Maybe, living permanently in that psychological "next year" we are so noted for — along with better crops, better jobs, and a better chance to make things better — they're always already one step into the future and so they never want to finalize anything.

It is easier, somehow, to say, "See ya!"

So, "See ya!" says the letter carrier as he turns to click crisply down the steps of your front porch, though he knows good and well he will see ya again tomorrow not, for hasn't he just told you he's off for Beautiful B.C. at the crack of dawn and kicking the dust of the prairieland off his heels most thankful?

"See ya!" calls the Amway woman to a dour bachelor who has threatened her with dogs if she ever comes back on the place before hell freezes over.

"See ya!" say the cavalier young men to broken-hearted young women, knowing all the while how precisely they mean to avoid them.

"See ya!" said my dad from a hospital bed, when I made ready to leave, the last time ever I saw him. "See ya!" said I, knowing full well that I wouldn't.

"See ya!" say the folks at a Rosetown beer parlour, though you're just passing through and lost again and so have stopped in, not for suds but to get directions.

"See ya!" they say at Swift Current Co-op, though you've just told them you're on your way to Thailand a week after you get home to Manitoba.

*See ya!* means: See you again by the grace of God and the absence of Spring floods or late and killing blizzards. *See ya!* means: See you again if I don't kill myself tomorrow because of no mail from back home and no rain and far too many grasshoppers. *See ya!* means: I won't walk alone when I leave you because I'll be thinking of saying *Hi* again next week or next year. Or far into the next better lifetime.

*See ya!*

# Pigweed, Pigs, and Other Pretty Surprises

Pigs are amusing in television shows made in New York or Hollywood, and recently there was a farm show on the colour-box to prove that nowadays your very neighbour might be raising pot-bellied foreign-gened porkers for people to pay a lot of money for and then play with. But pigs were not raised as laughable pets in Saskatchewan when I was younger, I can guarantee you that. Oh, now and again some hardy sow's litter would include a runty mismanagement of genes which was often offered by the man of the place to the woman of the kitchen who would tuck the bit of a creature into a cardboard box lined with straw and somebody's worn-out pyjamas or longjohns from the rag bag. The whole business was then placed behind the stove to keep it warm and to save Miss, or Master, Piggy from pneumonia. Sometimes it was the stove's oven that became the preemie's nursery; then once in a great while

— though not often confessed, save after a long night of cards and a long bracing bottle — somebody would slam the door without thinking and build up the fire for lunch, and . . . well . . .

Pigs are only incidental to this story. That's about the only way pigs *are* incidental, for if you have a pig on the place it usually knows how to be priority plus; if you have a pig barn full of them they are priority plus even above the eating and sleeping habits of the foolish folks who give them board and room — and sometimes even radio or TV entertainment. It's not just houseplants that get crooned to or fiddled at nowadays.

That's about it for pigs just now. Pigs are in this story mostly to bring us around to pigweed, for I've been wondering, while picking a mess of it for my supper, why it is called *pigweed* in the first place.

On my dad's farm, true enough, it flourished best in the vicinity of the pig barn — one supposes, for obvious reasons. But then again, maybe it was called, by most Saskatchewanians, *pigweed* because pigs were as fond of it as people were, only the pigs didn't have to go to the bother of washing the greens in three sets of water, perishing cold from a deep well, and then bringing a big kettle half-full of frigid aitch-two-oh to the boil on top of a great thumping-hot wood stove inside a tiny kitchen before tossing in the greens.

Drained, plopped steaming hot on top of boiled potatoes, laced with yellow-gold butter from a Jersey cow and sprinkled with salt and pepper, you needed only a boiled egg or two besides to make a fine and healthy dinner. At my mother's house, most people added a bit of vinegar to such a plateful, dribble, dribble, dribble, from the Woolworth's pseudo-cut glass vinegar cruet I never once saw run dry in all the years I lived under my mother's roof.

Maybe it's only we local yokels who call pigweed pigweed. You can't find it in your *Funk and Wagnalls*, even the so-called "Canadian version"; you look for it in vain in *A Dictionary of Canadianisms* or in the origination of phrases books. In fact, you will frustrate your prairie soul trying to locate it anywhere, maybe, unless you have an old version of *An Illustrated Guide to Prairie Weeds*. And the worst of it is, the iron-rich, spinachy weed my family and I, along with a lot of others, have always called *pigweed,* is not the pigweed of *An Illustrated Guide to Prairie Weeds,* which cost twenty-five cents from

Line Elevators Farm Service in 1941, it is really "lamb's quarters."

The Latin name for lamb's quarters means "white goosefoot." Who'd have thought they had ordinary common denominator geese in Rome when they were building colosseums — or *colossea* — and empires and a language for twentieth century doctors and Oxford scholars back in Caesar's good old days?

The weed book says lamb's quarters are called "white goosefoot" in Latin because the leaf looks like the flat of a goose's foot. It does, too! And the underleaf is white-ish. I'd have said "silver."

Years ago, when somebody who thought they knew the right name for pigweed laughed at me for calling it by the wrong name, in my determined German Lutheran way I decided I'd never be made fun of again about that, and from then on I called pigweed "lamb's quarters," even in my head — which knows how to keep shameful secrets and would not have snitched on me had I slipped on the inner into old patterns.

Then, somewhere down the road, some smallish farm child said to its mother in my presence, rather loudly, "She calls pigweed *lamb's quarters!*" He followed this with a full-breathed snicker of wonderment and I noticed his mother was trying to hide a smile.

Which just goes to show you, there are not nearly as many illustrated prairie weed guides gracing prairie homes as there are green-growing weeds illustrating the fields and pigpens of the same prairies.

The pigweed that the *Guide* calls "pigweed" is not the pigweed of that young Saskatchewanian, his mother, or my mother and me and a whole lot of other folks from back in the old days; it is really redroot and is not edible — unless maybe by pigs. Or geese. I'm so confused by now I'd believe anything. It is a native of tropical America so what the heck it was doing in my dad's dry sandy loam pigpen is beyond me.

To complicate the issue further this redrooted pigweed is closely related to the Goosefoot family, only its goose feet are dirty and will run you into trouble if you don't lop them all off before the plant makes seed. The *Guide* warns you, in biblical poetics, that this rascal will "be fruitful and multiply."

I can vouch for that.

It's the same with purslane or garden portulaca. When I first met the fleshy, waxy, long teardrop-shaped leaves of the garden portulaca I was beguiled by its prettiness and obvious hearty good health. It was in my first garden.

A neighbor warned me to pick it out by hand and burn it, for it stoutly refused to be hoed to the death and would regenerate overnight even if left in the hot July sun on a wilted lettuce leaf.

I thought she had over-put the case. But a couple of years later, having dutifully picked the current crop of portulaca by hand, I deposited it in a flat cardboard box, open to the sun, at the end of June, in the back alley for the autumn garden garbage pick-up in the tiny town where we were living.

We went away for the summer. When we got back, early September, the weed had put roots through the cardboard box and was greenly thriving.

The weedy garden portulaca or purslane is related to the fleshy ornamentals with gorgeous flowers, a favourite of many. The twenty-five-cent weed guide quoted earlier claims that apart from such ornamentals the whole purslane family is a downright dead-beat, as "it includes no plants of apparent use to man."

I have news for the *Guide*. Garden portulaca makes a succulent and very interesting addition to a green salad. Only don't add dressing until just before you eat, or you'll be sorry. Try it out for yourself, if you want to know why; I don't want to use, in print, for all the world to see, a favourite word from "You Can't Do That on Television."

You can learn a lot from illustrated guides to this and that in the days Father Time gives you for living, but you can learn a lot from people too, and sometimes I try to.

I met this charming woman once who seemed to me to be a transplant here from Venus or Saturn — or at least from some softer dimension — because she said she'd never ever in her life killed off a dandelion.

She *liked* dandelions, she said. They were beautiful and hardy and prolific, she said. I had not known that to be a plus factor in a weed. And besides, she said, you could eat them.

If only, she said, market garden asparagus was as hardy and industrious as dandelion greens, it wouldn't cost you four dollars and thirty-nine cents a pound to get a dose of your early spring vitt-amins.

She said "vitt-amins." I thought *that* was charming too.

And after that she told me she had never once, in all her life, killed a dandelion.

I was at the moment engaged in the third day of a laborious and ongoing war to regain my front yard from those not-so-charming yellow heads. But I stopped to consider that information and to present to mind the possible reasons for it being so.

Of course the charming woman had six children and lived on a farm with numerous goats and dogs and horses all presumably requiring currying and milking and feeding and spaying and et cetera. And she was helping her husband build this brand new house out of their old one.

And they had six children.

And her name wasn't Gertrude.

As for me, I had only two children at the time. Right now I haven't any. At least any who are children, if you take my meaning. And in other categories of the housewifely trade I have always said I'd rather live in a tent or a cardboard box if I couldn't move into a house that was already built. Old or new, it didn't matter, so long as there was no sawdust being made anywhere in the house while I was making stew or porridge in the kitchen.

Although we owned a farm, of sorts, it was small and safely out of the way in another part of the province. Which is where it was going to stay, as far as I was concerned, along with any hypothetical dogs and goats and horses.

All of which meant that, at least at that time, I had a lot more time than that charming woman to spend with the yellow enemy, and to learn to want to kill them.

If you live on a farm, as that woman did, you can call your soul your own, and also your dandelions. That is to say, if you want to grant freedom of expression to an acre and a half of front yard, you can do so without first arranging for a conference call with the neighbors to discuss it.

But if you live in a small town — which I did, at the time — it is a different story. You can be absolutely charmed by dandelions, if you like — dandelions to admire or to eat or to make wine out of or to test small children under the chin with to see if they still like butter. Nobody will stop you.

But if you permit those dandelions to flutter beyond the butter stage and flit on gossamer wings in the next high wind to spread yellow butter in the coming years to the rest of the village, it will get to be embarrassing.

Not that the good and kindly people in your good and kindly little Saskatchewan town will take you to task about it. What I mean is, people with six children for whom they sew all the clothes even to the stretchy underwear, people who are helping their husbands make brand new houses out of old ones, will just sort of stroll over to your place some evening, still wearing their carpenter's aprons and with pencils still behind the ear and kindly smiles on their faces.

And they'll offer, very kindly, to help you kill your dandelions. As you are obviously too busy — they can quite, quite understand it — to do the job yourself.

So when do you want it done, eh?

It's kind of awful when your name is Gertrude and so you are obliged to be a fighting spear maiden for all of your natural life.

If you are one of the Lutheran kind you have been taught a certain discipline. It says that you must not let your good and kindly neighbors do your personal dirty work. And so you somehow find the time and energy and whatever else is needed to get out there and do it all yourself.

There is nothing really charming about it.

I am older now than I was when I met the woman who believed in live-and-let-live, even when it came to dandelions. And I live, if not on a full-fledged farm, at least on a lot of acres far enough from neighbors who might have the time and inclination to watch my dandelions grow.

I sometimes watch them myself. Also the pigweed and purslane and lamb's quarters and Russian thistle and tumbleweed, taking a hand scythe to them occasionally when the body's biceps are getting a bit too flabby from courting the computer instead of the wood saw for too many days on end.

Since I am a lot less Lutheran than I used to be, I would be a relatively happy woman, cohabiting, as it were, with the entire compendium of a richly living illustrated guide to prairie weeds in the book of nature that surrounds me.

If it weren't for that dratted spear grass!

Unless you pull on your cowboy boots every time you want to go out the door here, your ankles are forfeit. And it takes thirty minutes every night before you go to bed just to "pick out" your socks.

There is absolutely nothing charming about *that, either!*

So I gave up on the names of the growing things that grace my scrub brush domain and jolly well just pick the darn stuff and eat it or mow it down with the scythe and then forget about it;

I am too old to be ashamed anymore of my misuse of the language.

Anyway, as far as pigweed is concerned, I feel a certain empathy for a green-growing thing for which the general population has to call in three animals to name, when "spinach weed" would have done the trick more efficiently.

As for the poor old pig, it gets to be a *hog* or a *porker* or a . . . well, let's not get started on that!

# The Power of Deer

The last thirty years or so we have heard more about power from the media than we have from the people and companies who are supposed to supply it to cook our dinners and heat or cool our houses. And quite rightly so, I suppose: everybody and his dog wants to claim power and then tell us all about it. But we have heard nothing at all on the subject from the all-knowing deer.

We have heard about Red Power, about People Power, about Grey Power and Black Power, Small People Power and the Power of those who require Oversize in their undies and aprons and are proud of it. But no one has written manifestos or treatises about Antler Power and neither Barbara Frum nor Oprah, to my knowledge, has ever interviewed a deer.

The deer has a power that perhaps only those on a disciplined spiritual journey will some day be required to recognize. It might happen just as the seeker's arrow finds the heart of the deer; it might happen while the seeker's knife slices venison or deer's heart for her family's supper or for her solitary own. It might happen while the seeker's secret heart is calm and whole and there is no deer nearby at all with either a soundly beating heart or with a jagged pierced one.

The power of the deer is as sure and silver-white and singing as the power that made them, made us; and it is as unexplainable. As the saying goes, You had to be there.

### Hunted

> One day we spied a young deer in a thicket
> Hard by the trail, when we were after meat;
> Head all erect, and body all a-wonder,
> He pattered here and there on nervous feet.
> His yearling hide shone yellow in the sunshine.
> Oh, he was flesh and blood like me! And soul.
> "Don't shoot! Don't shoot!" The sound of tearing thunder:
> In his wild heart — and mine — a jagged hole.

I was there. This was in the days when I lived with a hunter and trapper. The one who hunted deer for meat, the one who brought down the yearling. He came, in the last ten years of his life, under the power of the deer, and venison then no longer blessed the deep freezer at our house.

As a reward for having learned his lessons so well from the deer, the power-of-all-things brought that same hunter back to the earthly sphere once he had translated from his body and been "retrained" in other realms; brought him back as a teacher for someone who had loved him; brought him back repeatedly in his power-spirit form after he had translated to wiser realms and so should have been spared all that.

He came first in pictures-of-the-mind, with the deer. They flowed through the dream worlds shown on the inner screen when you are quietly serene and trusting; they came, in a way, in the kind of dream that steals in by day almost unnoticed while you are weeding turnips, but also in the kind of dream that thunders in during sleepless and troubled nights.

Always, those times, deer and ideas of deer poured through the consciousness, danced on the inner picture screen, talked to me out of poems and out of images in books. Became so real, in fact, that sometimes I could almost see them with my eyes open, as they danced and skittered and went about their business in the half-light of the room where I had my bed.

It was during that time I have now learned to label "the long dark night of the soul," the time when the Hound of Heaven pursued me as relentlessly as ever it had the early poet who coined that particular phrase for the focused power of the Originator-of-All-Things. The harrying power of this Originator, once Its quarry has sniffed at the bait of all-knowledge but is once again on the scurrying run, is not to be described by any poet, priest, shaman or yellow-clad Saskatchewan deer hunter. I can attest to that.

Words will not do it, and yet, somehow, there are those who have been clobbered by the power of the intelligent Force that has hunted us down to tell us It *is* the same power It has *given* the deer. What has been given the deer is final and terrible power over those who hunt and kill it without first asking *the deer's* permission. There are no words to describe or to explain that kind of power, and yet there are those of us who will insist on trying to write that power (and our own individualized experience of it) into words.

John Masefield, talking about the way to truth and about the need to express what one has discovered about it, puts it this way in his *Shakespeare and the Spiritual Life*: "He (that is, 'the great poet') apprehends truth by power:

the truth which he apprehends cannot be defined, save by a greater power, and there is no greater power." I would really have preferred to omit the last phrase, and very nearly did, on the grounds that it was going to get in the way of my own premise here, but that would have been tampering with the truth as apprehended by John Masefield. Who was touted, at least in my schooldays, not just as a great poet, but "one of the greatest." But that does not mean it may be presumed that Masefield had looked into the future and by that term was including himself.

But I digress — as a million digressors have expostulated, including Dorothy's Ma on "The Golden Girls." Not too far afield, but I digress. It would be relatively easy to fuzzify an earnest inspection of the power of deer by insinuating that what it really comes down to is an inspection *of truth*. Along the lines of: Truth is Power; Power, Truth. But that simply won't wash, when you try to make the pictures for Truth, for Power. It's true that dealing in abstract words — the words that refuse to make clear pictures in the mind — is easier for most of us in this age of convoluted speech than is the use of the plain and simple words any grade four seeker of truth can understand.

So, the way I see it, is this: There is a power that is inherent in the deer and its ways, and that power can enter the human mind and heart and lend clout — strength and verve, magic and vitality and the willingness to give — to anyone who has recognized those same qualities in the deer.

The power comes from being so in tune with one's place in the scheme of all things that one has chosen to be a wordless deer rather than a human being whose head is always cluttered up with words and, therefore, with schemes and machinations — including how to get a deer's head on the den wall or parts of its body on a hot platter on the dinner table.

That power has been recognized by some people — the original "Canadians" who lived in harmony with the earth, the Mother of All, and who, before going out on the hunt, solicited the spirit of the deer to present its body to the hunter's arrows so that its human brothers might live through another day or another winter; the hunter of today, who looks through the power scope on his deer rifle one morning directly into his target's eyes and then puts up his gun because of what he has seen there — the willingness of the deer to give its life into the hunter's hands.

I know, I know, many will see this all as nothing but stuff and nonsense, but that's OK, it doesn't change things for those who have been ready to receive the blessing of knowing the magical and sacred way things really are. That "knowingness," again, is so hard to put into words. So difficult that the One who is the symbol for the so-called Christian world had to tell *parables* to illustrate it, as did every other enlightened being including the best known buddha, the Gautama, to help us see the light. Blessed indeed is the patient one who has learned to hear and to recognize the power of the Originator-of-All-Things, the all-intelligent Force that allocates the power of the willingness to give, not to mankind but to the deer!

Power has a sound. Poets have tried to describe it if they have been blessed enough to have travelled to the realms of spirit-mind where the sound of power dwells — to that gold and white and hot-silver sounding ocean of power and, thankfully, of mercy. Yeats heard it, he has told me so in dreams; Whitman too; maybe Masefield, but I am not sure of that; the Sufi poets, surely. Many have travelled to those bournes and have heard there the sound and seen there the white hot light, but it is the poets who have had the courage to report it in terms and symbols other than those of the religions of their day.

Sometimes they were not poets — not even priests or saints or shamans — those who flew, as soul, to the silver-white ocean of energy that is the Originating power. Sometimes they were ordinary people who wound up there, temporarily, from a hospital operating room table; sometimes they were ordinary people with an extraordinarily fearless and experimental turn of mind — and with a terrible *need* to know. They reported blue stars visiting them in the darkness of a swiftly-traversed tunnel, the sound of the buzzing of bees about the head. Others have reported symphonic music heard through the fluttering leaves whilst all alone in the woods, or a white dazzling light that turned night to day for a while. There have even been those who can vouch for the perfume of flowers within the sterile environment of a recovery room. And along with these phenomena there is reported an overwhelming feeling of an energy, a force — a *power* that is all-accepting and all-*giving*. Some have called it *grace*.

The power of the deer. The "knowingness" that you are no more one thing than you are the other: you are no more deer than you are the being who needs to eat of your flesh in order to live, and so — if there is a mutual awareness of this connection — the willingness to give is axiomatic.

When the shoe — better, the hoof — is on the other foot, so to speak, you get No Hunting signs and people who would rather replant fifty evergreens every year than shoot the deer who nibble them to death even though they do not like the taste and so leave rings of spat-out end-buds around each young tree to prove it.

Where deer and humans recognize each other's right to be in the same place you hear from a long-time, old-times neighbour, "I feed the deer and the deer feed me and I'd like to see the government that can change that!"

William Faulkner has tried to deal with all this in his stories about the ties that humans have to the land they are born into, about the ties of the deer to that same land, and about the blood bond that binds the human to the deer. It is "the power of the blood," you might say. And if you see anything sacreligious in putting it that way, then I'm afraid I have not been clear enough.

Let me try. The power of the willingness to give up the self — to others, or to the soul-of-the-self — has nothing whatever to do with religion or with saviours, except insofar as a saviour presents himself/herself/itself as *an example* of the willingness to give up the self.

The Sufi poets, as I have speculated earlier, seem to be among those who have "been there" — to some realm or dimension or plane of consciousness where they have had the experience of "knowingness" accompanied by the light and sound reported consistently through the ages by those who have similar experiences. Their poems are a golden attempt to try to put it all into words to help the rest of us travel to those eternal realms too.

Jalal ad-Din, one much revered by the Sufis themselves, has put it this way:

> Awhile, as wont may be,
> Self I did claim:
> True self I did not see
> But heard its name.

Connect with the word *heard* please, and consider it after you have gone to bed tonight. If you begin to hear a faint electrical sound, as of bees murmuring around a distant hive, don't get up and look up the names of ear doctors in the phone book. Instead, give thanks that you have reached an extremely sophisticated level of awareness and are hearing the sound of self. It has been called, in other times, the sound of holy spirit. It has been called that by saints and others caught up in man-made religions who have become sharply aware of the sound of originating power by the simple, although rash, expedient of flagellation of the body — utterly unnecessary, by the way — or through such means as the wearing of a hairshirt.

If hairshirts make the body suffer as much as does rock wool insulation, I'm one of those who would forego enlightenment for a thousand reincarnations, I can tell you, rather than put up with it. Even one's *own* hair that has sifted its way sneakily down into the T-shirt or undershirt, I've found, after a trip to get the apian hair shaved off the back of the neck at a barber's, is downright unbearable; once, in fact, after such a shearing, I nearly put the car — to say nothing of myself and a hitch-hiking passenger — into a muddy ditch while trying to gain relief from the colony of black ants that seemed to be industriously employed in chewing out a new home in the small of my back.

It seems we have made here another digression.

Never mind, the poet's message bears repeating:

> Awhile, as wont may be,
> Self I did claim:
> True self I did not see
> But heard its name.
> I, being self-confined,
> Self did not merit,
> Till, leaving self behind,
> Did self inherit.

To put it in grade four terms, each one of us human beings is a little bump on the whirling coil of energy that is made up of *every* thing there is in this world. (Well, all the universes, but let's keep it simple.) I see my little "bump" as being *myself*, and separate from all the other little bumps on the coil-of-all-things; you make the same mistake. We can't help it. No one has ever shown us the whole picture.

When we forget about this little bump we call "me" and just get busy being the coil, then — oh satisfaction of all satisfactions — we have inherited ... what? Why, *everything*, of course; *everything*!

That is what the deer "know," and that is the power of the deer.

Please don't write and ask me why I have not used the word *love* here. "Surely *love* belongs in it," you'll say. And I will have to answer, "Define me *love.*" The truth of it is I have purposely avoided using the word because it has become so cluttered with meanings, with feelings, with individualized inner pictures of what it is to the one who is saying it. *Love* is one of those abstract words again: it does not make precise pictures — or sounds, or smells, or tastes, either. So is *power* an abstract word, I agree, but I am trying to present a sensory experience here, about what I seem to have learned about a certain "brand" of it.

The word *love,* again, does not serve us well anymore, it seems to me, once we are on the fearless and experimental journey.

The kind of journey the knowing deer makes as it honours "your" rye field, "your" bushland with its presence and its power. The kind of journey that is uncluttered by awareness of the little protuberance called self, the kind of journey wherein one is content to be everything.

We can work towards such an awareness, if we want to. If it is our time to want to do that. "I think, and so I am?" Sorry. Descartes presumed to assume that the human being, in its most glorious potential, was encompassed in, and by, *mind.* What *soul* was, what *spirit* is, was somehow just lumped in there with the holy grail of *mind*; in fact, you will not find a word in the German language, for one, to differentiate between the words *mind* and *soul.* Perhaps it's time we did, though. Differentiate.

The mind can lead us down the garden path, partly because it's the nature of the beast, let's say. As humans, however, we've been conditioned to prize the prizes so-called civilized societies award to those who seem to possess highly efficient minds. We are only too glad to be led by the nose to further worship of that faculty.

"I think, and so I am?" How about, "I *know*, BECAUSE I HAVE BEEN THERE?"

There are enough people now who have been there, to the realms of originating power, and who have found the courage to tell us about it. If we were to expend the same amount of money that put humans on the moon into a methodical and unbiased analysis of the phenomena that now bear such names as Near Death Experience and Out of Body Experience we might, we just might, within another generation, be teaching to our children not the intricacies of power politics but the simplicities of the power of the deer.

The fact is, you can see the power and you can hear it. And it is yours to use. What was St. Francis seeing and hearing when he was alone in the forest and had bade no brother intrude upon him? One did, and heard and saw, and reported it.

*God is the light of the heavens and of the earth.* Supposing Sura (24:35-7) of the Koran is using the word *light* as an actual and verifiable report of something actually experienced by the speaker?

The Originating Power which is characterized by light and by sound was present for that venerable reporter and it is present today. It pours through the deer and the deer know it; it flows through us and we ignore it.

Sometimes at our very peril.

# Following the Bliss of Weirdos

There are lots of perfectly decent folks around here to write about, why do you have to pick a weirdo?"

Roughly, that's the opinion given by someone living in the vicinity of a particular "weirdo"; it's a quote, insofar as I remember it, from a book. The writer of the book was telling readers how the book got written — I hope I am recalling at least the "quote's" setting adequately. The writer was reporting on the reactions of some of the people who were once neighbours to, or whose parents had once been neighbours to, a man who, to put it mildly, did not live up to the idea of what prairie society in that day and age considered normal.

He was someone who offended his neighbors by going about his life in an "unrealistic" manner, doing things entirely *his* way.

Apparently, if you're Frank Sinatra you can get away with that. On the other hand, perhaps even Frank Sinatra would not get by with "my way" in rural Saskatchewan. At least in the rural

Saskatchewan of the early part of this century.

I have generalized. I sometimes feel cheated myself — though I always try not to — when somebody else generalizes in print about *any* kind of weirdo, let alone a Saskatchewan one. But I needed to generalize because otherwise there is this arduous obligation to try to find the book again and then read it through again to find the quote and so quote that quote correctly. And I might never find it again, that book, either in the storage files of my own over-crowded and cluttered attic of a head, or on the shelves of the public library.

So I am going to compromise between ethical obligation to be accurate and ethical obligation to satisfy natural curiosity. This, in deference to Chekhov's dictum to dramatists: "Never bring a loaded gun on stage unless you mean to fire it off." So I shall go so far as to say that the "weirdo" spoken about was a man who built a boat when he didn't really have to. And this, for pity sake! while he was living in the self-inflicted dry-dock of the south Saskatchewan prairies.

Of course, nowadays, what passed for a weirdo in the early days of this country doesn't seem so weird to us. We've been conditioned by weird wars and weird politicians and a whole clatter and clammer of *unusual* musicians and singers. So a man who builds a great boat miles from any water beyond his own farm well and a slough or two is not as weird anymore to a lot of us as he might be.

Particularly since there are more and more of us who seem to have an inner need to build — or otherwise make, or do — things that are not necessary, certainly not practical, and often downright foolish.

I mean to say: a house with seven walls! a painting called "Tasting the Pleasures" with nothing but coloured ears in it! Excuse me. Some background behind the ears. I'm sure there is a joke there, about washing and so on, but I refuse to pursue it.

I mean to say: moving to a little old house in dry sandy bush country when you are nearly sixty and there isn't enough water in the well on the place to give a kitten a good weekly wash, let alone yourself and the overalls that are going to be *de rigueur* garb for you for the rest of your life if you stay there.

The quote that may or may not be 100 percent accurate, the one about the man building a boat when he didn't really need to, was going around in my head this summer morning at six-thirty when I got up to close up the house against the coming heat of the day. Since I was up and the morning was still, and perfumed with clover bloom, and altogether glorious, I put on the overalls I had scoured the night before, along with me, in the still very new bathtub and went out to cut wood with a small bucksaw that is at least as old as I am.

Now, I do not really have to saw wood with that saw. I have a power saw — given to me for Christmas years ago at my earnest request — and I have also a son who knows how to use it safely and insists he wouldn't mind at all coming out here and zipping up enough wood in a couple of hours to boil a whole year's worth of coffee and porridge, which is about all that is worth boiling, in my opinion, in the hot days of summer, beyond one's temper when the weather man promises more heat again tomorrow.

But I refuse to have the wood cut for me.

Does the word *weirdo* seem to steal immediately into mind? Well, let's consider, before securely labelling the package, the case of an aging body suffered to sit unemployed too many hours at the computer just so that the mind can be employed and coffee and porridge pried from the hands of supermarket owners and thus made available for the boiling. And then perhaps it doesn't seem so weird anymore to cut wood yourself with an ancient wood saw when there are more efficient ways to do it.

This being the latest New Age of Enlightenment we're living in at present, even governments are promising to be kinder and more gentle, which is about as mystical — or, perhaps, *mythical* — as any government can get, it seems to me. All the same, a lot of people, as I've said before, are allowing their neighbours to have a need "to be different."

To let them be so, too, and to not judge or assess them. But since that has not traditionally been the case, I've been wondering, whilst cutting wood this morning, why that is so.

I've been taken up with several wonderings, for that matter: 1) Why should someone call someone else a weirdo, in the first place? 2) Why should someone want to write about a person so different from most of us so that he becomes labelled? 3) Why should people want to read a book about such a labelled one?

The easy answers are: 1) Someone within our midst who does not "fit in" makes us feel threatened, or at least uncomfortable. 2) Writers like to write about the unusual because people like to read about the unusual. Which seems to answer question 3), but doesn't.

And as to that, if you are among the many seekers-of-soul who have found an inner harmony with the premises put forward by Dr. Joseph Campbell, who has been repeatedly pronounced "the world's foremost authority on mythology," you already know why it doesn't. And, most likely, you also know where (some of) the answer lies.

Let us sidle towards that revelation.

Joseph Campbell went to his just reward in higher realms of consciousness in 1987, just about the time I began to meet him through his earlier books, not the ones you will find in every Coles from here to Zimbabwe. And, unlike my dilemma, mentioned earlier, regarding quotations from books, I can lay you out quotes *about* Joseph Campbell and his well-documented truths about the human spirit as well as quotes *by* Joseph Campbell on the same subject a lot more easily and accurately than the pseudo-quote that began this dissertation.

I can do that because Joseph Campbell lives not only in my head and heart but in books on shelves an arm's length from this IBM-compatible keyboard — and so, to do so would not mean many phone calls and several trips to town with the attendant requirement of exchanging overalls for garb a bit less picturesque.

Campbell speaks, over and over and over, about the need to "follow one's own bliss." The first time I read those words I was already into the eighth year of my own long dark night of the soul and I would have given my eye teeth for *joy*, never mind *bliss*. All you earnest seekers know there is a precise, if fine, difference.

I was still rooted in the needs of this world, of course. Still, as a Buddhist I have known once had it, "too interested in the strawberry whipped cream sundaes." So I could not know I was working against soul itself by wanting the things (mostly, wanting certain *people)* that soul neither wanted nor needed but which I had been conditioned by the earthly mind to insist I could not live without.

Let us — why not? — put it this way: if you are programmed to be desolate unless you are leading a partnered life, yet your soul has been a cloistered hermit for a thousand reincarnations, doesn't that spell trouble-with-a-capital-T? And not just in River City!

Supposing what your soul wants is to have you living alone in a little old house with a little old bucksaw and a lot of books. And many ghostly presences, voices you hear when you sit in peaceful silence, to help you — the "you" that has been conditioned and darkened by earthly needs — to learn what you cannot find in an over-busy life, or in books with however many quotable quotations.

So, rooted in the world and the needs of the flesh, if one may be permitted a little biblical phrasing here, I wanted to be happy. I kept reading about Joy and the books that promised it said I could have it if I would only do certain things: get "outside of " myself and work for others; get "outside of" myself and *live* for others; meditate; do spiritual exercises daily; do *physical* exercises daily; go to church; stay away from churches; et cetera, et cetera, et cetera, even *eck* cetera, as a little girl with a large vocabulary used to say sometimes when I lived elsewhere, among other people rather than surrounded by deer.

Having read the books, I tried a little harder. But, to tell the truth of it, my life was already full of most of the things the books said I needed in order to be happy. Including cheerful service to others, though perhaps it is not fitting for me to either assess or to say that.

I was so cheerful and so full of willing service that I hardly had time to eat or sleep when the incident I mean to tell you about happened. But when I was alone there was no Joy there eating off the same TV snack tray or falling into sleep upon the same pillow.

So one night I was lying sleepless, staring at the skylight of my bedroom in an old apartment house where I was living just then. I was staring at the stars peering in, here and there, through the schmuck of a pair of pigeons that had elected to be my alarm clock every morning.

And I said, out of nowhere, to Whomever or Whatever might be "out there" with the stars and willing to listen: WHERE THE HELL IS THIS JOY I KEEP HEARING ABOUT?

As clear as a bell, inside my head a merry voice announced: Gertrude, we thought you'd never ask!

And for quite a while I had Joy. I was happy.

Then after a while there seemed to be something "gone missing" again. I thought it was a man, but it wasn't.

It was soul. I hate to say it.

I was wanting to live life "according to the norm." To have and to do and to be what most people had and did and were. I sure didn't want to be anybody's conversational weirdo! Life was very, very full. Only it was empty.

And suddenly it occurred to me that part of what I was missing was that still, small, and *merry* voice inside the head. I began to listen for her. When you have had voices in your head off and on for a lot of years you get to know what the gender of the tone is. I intended, if I ever surprised her "in residence," so to speak, to give her particular *aitch* and then some.

But she eluded me. Or I had forgotten how to listen. Oh, there was lots of superficial "head talk," the kind most of us have whether we know it or not; whether we would like it or not if we did some day connect with it. But there was not a peep out of the one who had seemed to promise me Joy everlasting just because I'd finally had the good sense to ask for it.

Withdrawal of support services. That's the way soul operates when it has plans for the stubborn mind with which it shares a tough and energetic body.

Back to biblical reminders. If you come out of the so-called Christian ethic, remember all that "Why hast Thou forsaken me?" stuff. Well, it wasn't only that brightly shining One who had that test foisted upon him; a lot of us more-muddied strivers get it too. Over and over, when there is some sort of "test" to be passed on that goldarned principled ladder-of-spirit, bingo! withdraw the support services, all you angels of soul, and let's see how this latest travail goes over with our "chosen one."

It seems to be an axiom: when you are in trouble there is help presented by The System of All Things everywhere you go and everywhere you look. The codicil to the axiom seems to be: you'll likely be too dumb to recognize it.

I should speak only for myself. But anyway, about then it was that Joseph Campbell began showing up everywhere: on television, in book stores, on the "public service" programs of libraries and universities. And saying, always, "Follow your own bliss!"

Don't listen to what anybody else says, follow your own oriole, march to the beat of your own drum.

There's something wrong here, I swore. Well, to speak utter truth, maybe I swore a time or two before I said that. There is for sure and all something wrong here, I said next. Because more and more I have been going my own way, doing my own thing, until I am on the verge of becoming a weirdo. And yet I am not happy!

And from somewhere deep inside the heart — *not* the head! — from somewhere deep inside the heart the long-lost, super-cheerful, still, small voice piped up and said, "More bad news! Turn on the TV and listen!"

And there was Joseph Campbell again, but saying now *this* about the dratted bliss he'd been telling us so long to follow. I paraphrase, of course. Though I have looked it all up again in his books, I do not mean to quote 757 words by Joseph Campbell here even though he is "in the public domain" now as well as safely in the public Great Hereafter where he is less liable to sue misconstrued theses and spiritual truths, to the sorrow of the striving misconstruer.

Here's what he said, at least, to me: 1) *Bliss* does not necessarily mean Joy. As in happiness. As in a pleasurable feeling. Great! I don't know about you, but that's just what I need to hear on any blue day to make the sun shine again. 2) Therefore, following one's own bliss might well involve pain (for ourselves and also, even more unfortunately, for others who are sometimes as sure as they possibly can be that our bliss lies *with them* if we would only wake up and smell the coffee). 3) The definition for *pain,* on the other hand, seems to be — wouldn't you know it? — exactly what we've always been led to expect.

We have to break this text into several other paragraphs now, not because the rules of grammar have eluded me, but because the rules of paragraphing for Reader Interest take precedence always. To wit: Keep the first short unless you want the second to take a long long leave of absence from your presentation.

Therefore, 4) In spite of what theologians and philosophers of the Western world have been trying to promote through several "new ages," there is a *Mind*-one-of-us and there is a *Wisdom* (soul)-one-of-us. And they are not one and the same thing at all, at all.

In fact, 5), we come in fives. Each one of those five *us*'s is a sheath of conscious energy, so to speak. The first is the physical body. We can see it so no one bothers to argue that maybe we haven't got one. This first body needs food and is oriented towards the material. The second is breath. It fits in and helps without a lot of argument. The third is the mind body. It's the trouble maker. It is oriented to the pleasure and pain of the senses, including the pain of an empty stomach. (An empty mind — this intrusion is my personal, perhaps weird, opinion — sometimes causes a heck of a lot less pain than does an empty stomach, but a crammed-to-the-gills *full* mind, look out for that one!)

Number four body is the wisdom sheath. The wisdom *of the body,* take note: the innate — and intricate, and dazzlingly beautiful — "knowing" whereby a fertilized egg becomes a living human being and then, by some mysterious chemistry, "oversees" itself to the veriest atom. The wisdom that puts the body on automatic pilot sometimes and takes you at the wheel of your Toyota Corolla safely home a hundred and forty miles through highway traffic and small town RCMP patrols and when you pull into your driveway you say, "What? Here already? I don't remember going through Chamberlain or Yellow Grass or *anywhere* at all!"

The last of the five "bodies" is the sheath of, guess what? Of *bliss,* heaven be praised! Where rapture lies, waiting to be awakened. And, claims Campbell, each individual life is "a manifestation of rapture." *Rapture.* Oh-oh! Another chance to get led down the garden path of Campbell definitions, and with blinkers on.

Oh well, in for a penny, in for a pound. The last point: *Rapture* means cheerful and willing eagerness to live life to the fullest *in spite of* pain and sorrow and anguish. *Pain* and *sorrow* and *anguish,* darn it, mean pain, and sorrow, and anguish.

I knew a poet once who, years ago, laid that last point out for my subsequent learning. He already knew it. I supposed he was just telling a sympathetic ear his latest love story. (Poets seem to have numerous.) He drove half-way across a continent to tell a woman he loved her.

In the way of Gawain, when he stops being a "lady's knight" the day he is just cantering along up a hill and suddenly comes across his true lady sitting with her horse and minding her own business. Beggar the fact that she says *No.* Beggar the fact that she doesn't want to hear any more about it, ever.

And, said the poet, all the while he was running gas into the back end of a little car and out again as blue exhaust, somebody inside his mind kept saying: You're going to get hurt again; you're going to suffer again! And *he* said: I don't give a good goddam, I'm going to her anyway!

He was following his own bliss, Campbell would say. In spite of pain and sorrow and anguish. He knew where lay the door to rapture. Which does *not* mean, I am sorry to say, that he somehow knew he was going to get the girl or, should he get her, get to keep her.

That man, whether he knew it or not, was, in Campbell's terms, "rooted in rapture."

*Soul* — yours, and mine, and everybody else's (supposing there is such a condition as *possessing* soul, which, in my personal opinion there is not) — soul is rooted in rapture. And my buddy, the poet, was operating out of his soul sheath rather than his mind sheath, as most of us do. Because it was important enough just then for soul to refuse to have it any other way.

Soul is rooted in rapture. Campbell doesn't say it that way. But then, if we were to compile an entire, new, lexicon of Campbellese, we would easily discover, I contend, that what most of us mean by *soul* is what Campbell and the philosophers of the East call *the sheath of bliss.*

It takes discipline, this following of one's own bliss. Very often, what *I* want to do is to follow my own *mind.* We have heard, often enough, that a conditioned mind can make a very bad master and I am here to report in the affirmative. After sixty years of living securely within the mind it is most difficult to break the patterns.

All too often then, I do not want to take the opportunities that life presents because I know there will be pain involved, even if it is no more than the pain of possible failure.

I do not fear failure *as failure,* I'm pretty sure, but because as "unfinished business" a failed attempt has to be lived with — according to my mind patterns — over and over again. A dry hole water well; a job that demands more than you can give; a book manuscript that garners only rejection slips; a friendship that proves to have been only window dressing.

And yet, when I go against the gainsaying mind and do it anyway, something happens that is wonder-full. You do what has to be done, for example, to get a fifty-foot well sunk at fifty dollars the foot with nothing going right from the word *go* and with something new going wrong each hour of each day it takes to do it. Then, one night, the thing accomplished, you are standing outside on the doorstep, breathing the perfumes of drying alfalfa and clover, looking at the stars and being very . . . well, *joyful* — just for the moment, you understand. It is as if you are not there anymore. Not anywhere, unless it is within the heart of a star.

Then, zippo, you are back within the world of the physical — the body with its need for food and breath, the mind with its myriads of needs and its endless chatter chatter chatter. An hour has passed and it might have been a moment.

And you have one of the enlightenments you have read about in books and couldn't quite understand at the time. You suddenly "know" that you have been living in a state of rapture. Not just for the hour you were one with the stars and the stars were one with you and all of you knew it, but during the awful time just past when things were going wrong (and costing more money by the minute) and you were sure you would not live to see it through, but you followed through anyway, because there was no way out of it otherwise. Except to slash your wrists — not much of an option if you come from a long long line of non-slashers.

Come hell or high water, you follow through.

Some people follow through on a project that lasts long enough to make slashers of most who have not somehow begun to operate out of the soul body. It might be a rocky marriage or it might be a war or it might be selling groceries over a corner store counter when you wanted to be a doctor.

Because, the truth is, so many more people "follow through" in commonplace scenarios than do in the more dramatic ones. And since familiarity breeds contempt, so to speak, we do not see it as the stuff of song and story. To hang in there for forty years selling turnips and Vaseline and bread does not "sing" as does hanging yourself in your mother's front parlour because you could not go away to college.

When someone is following through with what he knows he *has* to do he does not necessarily know *why* he has to do it. If what he is following through on goes against the grain of common sense and the forbearance of his neighbors, why then our curiosity — as readers of this person's story as set out in a book, or as followers of our own bliss — is piqued, but definitely.

So. Maybe it's time for a recap.

I have been contending here that there are some human beings who have to do what they *have* to do. They *have* to pursue a course — no matter how painful or unpopular or how ludicrous or unrealistic — because the soul, for whatever its reasons, is demanding it.

Soul, by the way, in my experience, when it comes to giving reasons, always has — à la Jimmy Durante — "a milliona dem."

The followers of their own bliss, even if it is building a boat in landlocked Saskatchewan to sail home to the old country, have to travel their own particular, peculiar road. Most often, alone.

The mainstream of society tends to label such travellers *weirdos*. Or whatever label is popular at the moment. Those of us who are fascinated by them and want to hear, in as much detail as a researcher can dig up, the story behind the "craziness," are fascinated because our own particular and peculiar soul is signalling *to us* that there is something more that *we* have to learn. And that maybe it is our turn next.

The something we have to learn is this: Only when we have learned to accept pain with the same equanimity that we meet a balanced day, and pleasure the same way, only then have we passed through the door marked *Rapture* and are living securely — blissfully — within the worlds of soul.